Recommendations from Readers

Until Then is a book that should be read by every pastor and layman! It is a major contribution in the area of Christian stewardship. You quickly realize that the contents have been born in the heart of a real Christian steward. As he shares so ably the heartbeat of Paul he reveals his own deep commitment as a steward.

My feelings and convictions regarding the manuscript can best be described through several word pictures:

Scriptural - The book is truly scriptural - being confined mostly to the writings of Paul. The words of Paul are handled in a beautiful way. Every truth presented is based on specific Scriptures. The interpretations of the passages are excellent.

Theological - It gives a real scriptural basis for the theology of giving. The conclusions deduced from Scripture are theologically sound. Scriptural stewardship becomes so logical and so beautifully related to our Lord.

Sermonic - The book is a *must* for any pastor searching for fresh ideas and materials regarding Christian stewardship. The entire book is replete with sermonic material. Also the layman will find ample resources here.

Practical - It speaks to each of us where we are. The more I have reflected on "contentment" as the goal of stewardship the more I have realized the truth of this conclusion. Truly there can be no real contentment without real Christian stewardship.

Thanks, Doug Laird, for a major contribution in an area so vital to our own Christian contentment and to the conquest of this world for Christ.

— James E. Coggin, Pastor Emeritus
Travis Avenue Baptist Church
Fort Worth, Texas

As a pastor I am continually searching for new ways to communicate the vital concepts of Scripture to the contemporary scene. This is particularly challenging in the area of stewardship. I deeply appreciate any tool that can help others understand this "touchy" yet crucial aspect of Christian discipleship.

Douglas Laird has done a great service by putting just such a tool in the hands of inquiring individuals who grapple with this sensitive issue. It answers the tough questions in down-to-earth language we can all understand. May the Lord use this valuable resource to lead young and old alike on the exciting, fulfilling adventure of Christian stewardship.

— Michael D. Dean
Pastor
Travis Avenue Baptist Church

I believe that Doug Laird has few equals in the area of Christian stewardship. I have been fortunate enough to hear him lecture on the subject, talk to him personally about the Biblical teaching of stewardship, and review his writings.

Doug stays close to the Scripture with an ability to apply and illustrate the teaching in a very relevant manner. He writes and speaks, however, not just from the standpoint of a skilled teacher but also from the position of success experienced in his field. He has been blessed by God with an ability to lead people and churches into the grace of giving. We will probably never know what his leadership has meant to Christian education, evangelism, and missions.

— Ben Merold
Harvester Christian Church
St. Charles, MO

The word stewardship is stale to many people, even Christians. Read this book and you will find that stewardship is included in the word salvation and that it is exciting and joyful.

This book is well written and it brings new insights to familiar Scripture passages. It is a fresh study of the subject and leaves the reader with profitable instruction and inspiration.

In this last chapter, "The Goal of the Steward," the reader will find a surprise. The goal is contentment.

I recommend this book to all who are interested in finding the deeper meaning of the Christian life.

— H. Franklin Paschall
Retired Pastor
First Baptist Church
Nashville, TN

Former President
Southern Baptist Convention

Until Then . . .

The Apostle Paul on Giving and Contentment

Douglas L. Laird, Th.D.

Christian Stewardship Ministries

4606 North Perryville Road
Litchfield Park, AZ 85340
1-800-926-4891

ISBN: 1-883748-00-3

All Scriptures marked (KJV) are from the *King James Version* of the HOLY BIBLE (originally published in 1611).

All Scripture quotations marked (NEB) are from *The New English Bible.* Copyright © The Delegates of the Oxford University Press and the Syndics of the Cambridge University Press, 1961, 1970.

Scripture quotations marked (NIV) are from the HOLY BIBLE *New International Version*, copyright ©, New York Bible Society.

Scriptures marked (RSV) are from the Revised Standard Version of the Bible, copyrighted 1946, 1952, ©1971, 1973.

Scripture quotations marked Phillips are reprinted from J. B. Phillips: *The New Testament in Modern English*, Revised Edition. © J. B. Phillips, 1958, 1960, 1972., published by Macmillan Publishing Co.

Dedication

This book is dedicated to Prue's and my wonderful grandchildren. Steve's children: Jacqueline and Rebecca; Jan Cunningham's children: Scott and Christine; and Phil's children: Shaun, Tiffany and Ashley. I pray that they will learn and live by the wonderful concepts contained in this book.

Contents

Preface

Here I have avoided compiling the works of others who have written on Paul or quotations from commentaries available to any who wish to do a verse-by-verse study of Paul's Epistles. Instead, I have written what could be understood and appreciated by the casual Christian layman, as well as the more serious Bible student.

For the benefit of the former, care has been taken to point out those finer points of textual emphases but without tedious and often tiresome detail. It is hoped the serious student will also discover the reading rewarding, and that both he and the more casual reader will find the reading both inspirational and illuminating.

One of the most exciting dimensions of Paul's fuller treatment of stewardship is the accomplishment or the reaching of the goal either subtly or aggressively sought by many — contentment. No study of Paul's ministry and teaching should overlook his emphasis on dedication that leads to or develops in one that noble and sought-after grace of contentment.

But it must be remembered that stewardship is not a "spectator sport." Appreciation and growth are found only in participation. So, my greatest joy will be achieved if readers will either expand what they are doing or begin what they have neglected. To that end, and until then, it is sent forth with my prayers.

Douglas L. Laird, Th.D.

Introduction

In his enthusiastic attempt to dramatize the second coming of Christ, a minister recently commented to his congregation, "If I knew that Jesus would return in seven days, my wife and I would go out and buy on credit everything we could think of and wanted and would enjoy it all for the week. Then when Jesus came and took away His own, we would leave it with them." His words probably provoked a lot of mental response, but it totally missed the proper attitude for the believer and the teachings of Paul on stewardship and discipleship.

I believe if I knew Jesus would return in seven days, I would endeavor in that week to give to the needy everything I had — even the chairs on which we sit — lay up treasures in heaven, and shout His praises as I went out to meet Jesus, with no "goods" or "things" in my hands.

That was Paul's method. Even as he spent his last days in a Roman prison cell, his poverty, after a life of stellar accomplishments, was reflected in his request that Timothy would bring the coat Paul had left at Troas and hasten to arrive before the winter cold chilled his body. What a way to go!

This should be no surprise to the student of Paul because stewardship, according to Paul, was unmistakably linked to the fact and extent of one's relationship to Jesus and the subsequent and inevitable relationship to himself and those about him. Paul was willing to count "all things but loss for the excellency of the knowledge of Christ Jesus" (Phil. 3:8), and until His return, he would live that he might apprehend, or lay hands on to achieve, that for which he was apprehended of Jesus Christ (Phil. 3:12). Until then, he would live as a steward of His Lord.

Paul's personal stewardship commitment seems to be reflected first in his statement made while on the Damascus road, "...Lord, what wilt thou have me to do?" (Acts 9:6, KJV), and finally expressed in his summary exhortations to the Ephesian elders whom he gathered about him en route back to Jerusalem after his third missionary journey. He had not coveted another's goods (Acts 20:33). He had provided for himself so God would be glorified in the hearts of the people without their thinking he had used his position for personal benefits (Acts 20:34). He had taught the people to share the fruits of their labors with those who were weak (Acts 20:35). He had found the blessedness of a mind that longed to give instead of a mind that longed to receive (Acts 20:35).

The last of these is a concept which one wonders if Paul had not quoted to himself again and again through the years because the truth of this is found throughout his ministry. There are so many expressions of Paul's giving, even to his being ready to be offered up to God, as found in his last letter to Timothy yet, there is not a single occasion when he contended for what should be done for him, unless one so reads 2 Corinthians 12:11 where he speaks of due commendation. However, I see neither that statement nor Philemon 19 as emanating from a heart that desired to receive. His words and deeds reflect instead a life lived for one purpose: to give that others might live. Paul's words to the Philippians, "to me to live is Christ and to die is gain" (Phil. 1:21, KJV), indicate that Paul obviously understood genuine stewardship.

Even though Paul often wrote in a tightly organized style that characterized the Greek mind, his words on stewardship elude efforts to pull out and exhibit them in such neatly organized forms. Perhaps that should be no surprise to us. Stewardship was merely a part, albeit an important one, of the larger emphases in his instructions or his sharing with the believer. It saturated his commitment and therefore is a part of all his writings. So, with a subtle fear of oversimplification, I shall first deal with what Paul saw as the basic concepts of giving.

−1−

Finding The Road Map
Basic Concepts of Giving

With the coming of Jesus Christ, the promised Messiah, a new age was ushered into human history. That age will give way to an eternal age when Jesus comes again. Until then, believers are entrusted with the stewardship of God's resources. What is the believer's task? What role should be performed? What actions should be taken?

No person has spoken to these issues more ably than the Apostle Paul. Hence, I have taken a mental journey through his writings to find answers. I invite you to follow where my mind has been led as we discover the believer's role as a steward of the riches and grace of God.

Glorify God

Until Jesus' return, the believer's stewardship relation or purpose is to glorify God. Erecting buildings, paying missionaries, or feeding the poor find purpose only as they glorify Him. Paul contended that, ". . .whatsoever ye do in word or deed, do all in the name of the Lord Jesus, giving thanks to God and the Father by him" (Col. 3:17, KJV), and this he passionately practiced in the unfolding of his own life. On numerous occasions Paul claimed to have worked with his own hands to provide for his needs. That was done in order to avoid criticism from those he might have asked for support and for fear that all possible glory might not have been given to God (Acts 20:33-35; 2 Cor. 11:9; 1 Thess. 2:9; 2 Thess. 3:8).

As he encouraged the Corinthians to follow through with their giving to the needs in Jerusalem, Paul expressed a far deeper fullness of purpose in their giving than simply meeting a physical need of the poor. The primary end result would be: it would bring glory to God.

> This service that you perform is not only supplying the needs of God's people but is also overflowing to many expressions of thanks to God. Because of the service by which you have proved yourselves, men will praise God for the obedience that accompanies your confessions of the Gospel of Christ, and for your generosity in sharing with them and with everyone else (2 Cor. 9:12-13, NIV).

But I confess that the word "glorify" is a very troublesome word to me. After all, how does one glorify the "all glorious?" How do we bring glory to Him who is altogether glorious? Perhaps for us, it would be understood best by the word "honor" instead of "glorify." "Honor" seems to translate better into the actions of man to God. How does one honor the Lord? Maybe this can be understood more clearly by asking the question, How does one honor his parents? They are who they are, and the son is who he is. How, then, does the son honor his parents? I think you know. The son honors his parents by what he does, what he says, what he accomplishes, and by doing that which pleases his parents. Conversely, one dishonors his parents by what he does and who he is. Likewise, we glorify or honor God by who we are and what we do. We glorify Him by reflecting His thoughts and will and love and mercy and forgiveness and unselfish giving. God is a giver, and we glorify Him when we give in the spirit of His giving.

Accomplish the Goal of Redemption

Until then, the believer's stewardship relation or purpose is to accomplish the goal of his redemption. Why was one saved? I know that we could truthfully and appropriately answer that God gave His Son who paid the price to redeem us from death. But is it no more than that? Is the whole purpose of redemption to deliver as many as possible from hell and having done so, relax all intent and desire for those who have so obtained their salvation? Not according to Paul. He testified, "I press on to take hold of that for which Christ Jesus took hold of me" (Phil. 3:12, NIV). He believed that God had a purpose in saving or laying hold on him initially. His desire, first, was to understand that purpose and, second, to achieve it in his life. He would lay hold or accomplish that for which God had originally saved him.

The above lines are extremely meaningful to me. They sum up the purpose for the believer's existence, which is his stewardship accountability to God. Some years ago, I had these lines written in calligraphy and framed, and they now hang with other pictures in my office. I have fallen woefully short of the goal expressed in those lines. Yet, I feel that these words of Paul so perfectly express the desire of every believer — to lay hold on that thing or those things for which God laid hold on him.

But the question arises, "Why did God lay hold on me? What is God's will for my life? How can I pursue something unless I know what that something is?" Of course, the basic areas to which the Scriptures direct commitment are prayer, Bible study, moral rectitude, financial support, family care, and many others. And in all of these, there is that constant sensitivity to God's will and to effectively doing all those things in the time and manner which God designs for our lives. Yet, there are other areas that may be laid out in principle in the Word but lack the details essential for our lives. For example, there should be no question that the Bible teaches that mission work is the plan and purpose of God to reach the peoples of the earth, but only by the Spirit's leadership in the life of an individual is he or she convinced that it is God's will for him or her to be a missionary.

Faithful stewardship required of Paul that he consistently fulfill all those multifaceted dimensions of a life under the Lordship of Jesus. It also required that he determine the will of God in all those other and less clearly defined areas for which he was responsible to God.

Perhaps this is the background of Paul's words in Romans 12:1-2, in which he exhorted the believers that they "be not conformed to this world but be transformed by the renewing of" their "minds that" they. . ."may prove what is that good and acceptable and perfect will of God." They were not to prove the value, worth, or genuineness of the will of God. God's will did not need to be tested or proved, but the believer needed to prove to himself that God's will was all-sufficient for his needs. It was *good* — it was best for the believer. It was *acceptable*; it reflected that which God approved and was acceptable by God for the believer. It was *perfect* — it was complete; it left no part of the believer's life unattended. Thus, the believer can be assured that God's will is best for him; it reflects the desires, wishes, or purposes of God in his life; it is complete and leaves no part of his life without direction.

Paul's letter to the Colossians speaks of the perfection or completion in the will of God, saying, ". . . that ye may stand perfect and complete in all the will of God" (Col. 4:12, KJV).

So the Christian steward must first acknowledge the fact of the completeness of God's will for his life and then his total accountability to carry out God's purpose for every dimension of that life. This was Paul's concept of stewardship, whether it related to money or to any other part of one's life. And anything less than this is a fragmented, and perhaps I can say a "demented" kind of stewardship.

Such a stewardship does not distinguish between stewardship of money or stewardship of body or stewardship of time. Instead, all of life is that stewardship of faithfully fulfilling every dimension of God's purpose for His children.

One wonders at the profundity of Paul's words when he summarily wrote to the Philippians, "For to me to live is Christ, and to die is gain" (Phil. 1:21, KJV). Living was not for how much he could *get* but for how much he could *give*. The will of God was absolutely paramount to Paul. In his living, the name and will of Christ would live. No selfish purpose would distract from the plan and purpose of God in his life. To *live is Christ*, to *die is gain*.

Such a stewardship of will may provoke a negative response from some who would contend that such a blind loyalty is untenable and that none should be expected to give such an allegiance to anyone. But this kind of loyalty is the role of the believer. He is a bondslave. Jesus is Lord, and this should not suggest negative unpleasantness. Instead, it promises all those things deeply desired by everyone.

You see, the slave did not have a hand in determining the direction to go or the place to work. The master directed in that. Likewise, God, if in complete control of our lives, guides us in every step we take—vocationally and otherwise. Nor did the slave worry about his income or his provisions. That, too, was the master's responsibility. The slave could work without a single worry about food, clothing, and shelter. It was the master's concern to care for his slaves. The slave was not to worry about daily needs, hospital care, or even retirement. The master had that responsibility. The basic concerns of "Where do I go?" "What do I do?" and "What do I get paid for it?" are all cared for in our servant relationship to our Master. This is not bondage. This is freedom!

The child at play enjoys far more freedom and peace in a fenced-in yard than the child next to the street in an open yard where mother repeatedly shouts, "Come back from the street!" Granted, the rebellious child who tries to climb out of the yard is unhappy. I fear, though, that he is like the church member of whom the deacon remarked, "He has just enough sin to mess up his religion, and just enough religion to mess up his sin." But biblical stewardship is not reflected in rebellion to the will of God but in obedience to the will of God.

Conceivably someone would remonstrate, "But I do not have the strength to do that." Without going too far afield in Christian growth, let me remind you of Ephesians 3:20, "Now unto him that is able to do *all* we *ask*/ able to do *all* that we *ask* or *think*/ able to do *above all* that we *ask* or *think*/ able to do *abundantly above all* that we *ask* or *think*/ able to do *exceeding abundantly above all* that *we ask* or *think,* according to the power that worketh in us" (author's rendering and italics). Surely there would be no lack of strength after claiming that promise.

Building for the Habitation of God

Until then, the believer's stewardship relation or purpose is that he may be as a building "fitly framed together for the habitation of the Spirit" (see Eph. 2:20-22).

In fact, what purpose is a faithful stewardship except it be to provide an instrument for the working of God in the person of the Spirit within us? He is the strength for the believer; He is the joy of the believer; He is the comfort to the believer; He is the restraint to the believer; He is the assurance to the believer; He is the leadership for the believer. Indeed, He is God's presence with man, and one's response to the Holy Spirit inevitably reflects his stewardship response to God. A steward does not ascertain the will of God apart from the Holy Spirit who conveys it to him — he cannot be a faithful steward in the work of God without the enabling power of the Holy Spirit.

Therefore, Paul reminds the Ephesians that Jesus Christ was the Chief Cornerstone; "In whom all the buildings fitly framed together groweth unto an holy temple in the Lord: In whom ye also are builded together for an habitation of God through the Spirit" (Eph. 2:20-22, KJV). Whether this refers primarily to the church or to the believer, some significant truths emerge. (1) The building is made of many parts (v. 21). (2) The building is made of precut parts – "fitly framed" (v. 21). (3) The building is a growing structure (v. 21). (4) The building is for Divine habitation (v. 22). (5) The building has a Divine Architect (Eph. 2:20-22).

Paul conveyed that the building was a work of God and designed to be an abode for God whose purpose would be thwarted by an unfaithful stewardship of the people of God. Once again the picture by Paul is that stewardship is a faithful fulfilling of the will of God in the totality of one's commitment to God. I seriously doubt that the pieces of the habitation of God could be "fitly framed together" if there is an obstinate and selfish spirit in one's giving.

Maturing the People of God

Until then, the believer's stewardship relation or purpose is to develop and grow the people of God.

Surely there is not in any of us a calling or an ability to teach and develop the believers in the Word of God as did Paul, but no faithful steward will disclaim any and all responsibility to edify the brethren. We may carelessly want to apportion our time, talents, and money to satisfy the selfish guidelines set for ourselves. But Paul contended,

> For none of us liveth to himself, and no man dieth to himself. For whether we live, we live unto the Lord; and whether we die, we die unto the Lord; whether we live therefore, or die, we are the Lord's (Rom. 14:7-8, KJV).

So there is an accountability to God and subsequently to those about us, regardless of how small our abilities might be. And a sense of faithful stewardship might go a long way to correct irresponsibility in church attendance or the desperate pleading that often is done by the minister of education in an attempt to enlist teachers for Sunday School classes.

When Paul wrote to the Romans, he spoke of his desire to see the brethren there and continued, "often times I purposed to come unto you (but was let hitherto) that I might have some fruit among you also, even as among other Gentiles" (Rom. 1:13, KJV). Paul's stewardship of his entire life to God created in him an insatiable desire to develop others that they, too, would bear fruit to the glory of God.

This same concept accounted for his receiving and rejoicing in the gifts of the Philippians who gave unselfishly to the needs of his life.

> Not withstanding ye have well done, that ye did communicate with my affliction. Now ye Philippians know also, that in the beginning of the gospel, when I departed from Macedonia, no church communicated with me as concerning giving and receiving, but ye only. For even in Thessalonica ye sent once and again unto my necessity. Not because I desire a gift: but I desire fruit that may abound to your account. But I have all, and abound: I am full, having received of Epaphroditus the things which were sent from you, an odor of a sweet smell, a sacrifice acceptable, well pleasing to God (Phil. 4:14-18, KJV).

Beyond this, I shall not wander off into the mind-boggling dimensions of Paul's efforts by precept and example to grow, mature and influence for good the people of God. Suffice it to be stated that no study on the stewardship commitment of Paul would be complete without mentioning his commitment to influencing others to be more like Jesus. In fact, I suppose it could be said that that was his stewardship commitment.

−2−

I'll Walk The Line
Guidelines for Giving

No study on the purposes for stewardship commitment would be complete without a review of 2 Corinthians 8, where Paul gave at least nine reasons for one's giving to God of his material possessions. Perhaps another careful reading of the chapter would make these a bit more meaningful for the reader.

After the Example of Others

The believer should give because of the example to others (vv. 1-5). In his encouragement to the Corinthians to follow through with their commitment to help the needy saints in Jerusalem, Paul did not hesitate to encourage them by the example of the churches of Macedonia. And the example was more meaningful when he set it in the background of the material deprivation of the Macedonians.

They gave out of adversity − *"in a great trial of affliction" (v. 2).* − The *New International Version* translates their trial as "most severe." I fear that few, if any of us in today's society, can perceive the intensity of the suffering of these people. What a time for them to say, "Paul, we have our own troubles. Why should we be asked to give to relieve the troubles of others," but they didn't. It is no wonder that they were cited as examples. They gave out of adversity.

They gave with joy, "the abundance of their joy" (v. 2). —The NIV translates it "overflowing joy." Williams translates it, "the mighty flood of their gladness." And the *New English Bible* translates it "exuberantly happy." I confess that I labor the point but not without purpose, because this communicates a fact which is so foreign to the life-style of many but a point which should characterize the life-style of all. Instead of complaining about the offering or criticizing the preacher's sermons on giving, these people were ebullient with ecstasy. Can you imagine that! Sure you can because you know that giving as taught by Paul was cheerful *(hilaros)* giving (2 Cor. 6), not giving with delay and regret and scorn.

They gave with extravagance (vv. 2-3). —This is not to indicate that they gave large sums of money, but it reveals that in accordance with the level of their resources, they gave abundantly. Paul speaks of these people as being in "deep poverty," and yet they gave with "rich generosity" (NIV). The NEB translates it, "They have shown themselves lavishly open-handed."

It would have been so easy for them to have protested to Paul, "Brother, we are sympathetic toward your appeal for an offering for the poor saints at Jerusalem but you know how it has been with us lately. We just don't have it to spare. If times were better, we would be pleased to help and maybe later on we can but not now. But please know of our interest, and we do pray that God will be with you in your worthy effort." And in so doing, they would have excused themselves from the responsibility of giving and gone on about their usual course of life, but they did not. Instead, Paul described their giving as "going to the limit of their resources, as I can testify, and even beyond that limit" (v. 3, NEB). They were not trying to see how little they could give and be excused. Rather, they joyfully shared abundantly of what little they had.

They gave with intense desire. — They begged for an opportunity to share: "they begged us most insistently, and on their own initiative, to be allowed to share in this generous service to their fellow-Christians" (v. 4, NEB). The attitude of these early Christians would cause many of us to examine again our own attitude toward giving. They saw it as an opportunity not to be missed, rather than a misfortune to be shunned. How quickly they had grasped the timelessness of those treasures laid up in heaven and the futility of storing their treasures where moth and rust would corrupt and where thieves could break through and steal.

They gave with a personal commitment. — Contrasted to the Macedonians, there are so many today who equate commitment with financial support. By sending their money to the church, they feel that their need for church worship has been met. In giving of the abundance of their resources they rationalize that their duties in Christian service have been fulfilled. Their gifts indeed may have been sorely needed and have been used carefully, but how mistakenly people feel that after giving their gifts, there is no further need for them in the church.

It is no marvel that Paul used these Macedonians as examples for, as he said, "their giving surpassed our expectations; for they gave their very selves, offering them in the first instance to the Lord, but also, under God, to us" (v. 5).

To Prove His Love

The believer should give to prove his love. It would not be correct to declare that love cannot be expressed in any way other than giving, but it is certainly the natural way to express it. Out of love, parents give to their children. Out of love, children give to their parents. Out of love, a friend gives to a friend. Out of love, a sweetheart gives to a sweetheart. Out of love, a believer gives to God.

Surely Paul was evidencing to the Corinthians the love of the Macedonians when he wrote, "they urgently pleaded with us for the privilege of sharing in this service to the saints" (v. 4, NIV).

Their fellow believers in Jerusalem were in need. Paul had communicated their need to them, and it did not fall on deaf ears. Their salvation had created in them a spirit of unselfishness, and that spirit of unselfishness welled up in an "abundance of joy" at the opportunity to help the brethren, and they pleaded with Paul to let them participate.

Later in the same chapter, Paul chided the Corinthians, saying, "I am not commanding you, but I want to test the sincerity of your love" (v. 8, NIV). There really could not be love without response. The marquee at a Georgia church appropriately read, "You can give without loving, but you can't love without giving."

An intentional effort is made to avoid making reference to other biblical characters while endeavoring to review and draw conclusions from the writings of Paul. However, a quick reference to King David and his words about the raising of funds for the building of the Temple cannot be avoided. Before he made a gift of three thousand talents of gold and seven thousand talents of silver, which is no small gift even for a king, he explained the motivation for his giving: "Because I have set my affection to the house of my God . . . I have given to the house of my God" (1 Chron. 29:3, KJV).

It was explained to the Corinthians that Titus and two other brethren would be coming to receive their gifts and apparently Paul had spoken highly of the Corinthians to them. So Paul urged the Corinthians to be responsive in their giving which would support his claim that they indeed loved the Lord. There was no other badge or symbol which could as well signify the love of these Corinthians of whom Paul had spoken. "Wherefore show ye to them, and before the churches, the proof of your love and of our boasting on your behalf" (v. 24).

But no review of the heart of Paul, whose love expressed itself in giving, is complete without hearing him testify, "Brethren, my heart's desire and prayer to God for Israel is, that they might be saved" (Rom. 10:1, KJV), and coupled with this is his expression of inexplicable charity when he groans:

I have great heaviness and continual sorrow in my heart. For I could wish that myself were accursed from Christ for my brethren, my kinsman according to the flesh: Who are Israelites... (Rom. 9:3-4, KJV).

To Be Well-Rounded

The believer should give in order to be a well-rounded Christian. It is remarkable indeed to hear Paul denounce the sins and mistakes of the Corinthians and then to hear him laud the dimensions of their Christian development. "You excel in everything — in faith, in speech, in knowledge, in complete earnestness and in your love for us" (v. 7, NIV). For any believer to have the great Apostle pin that many medals on his chest is enough to make pride swell like a heated balloon. Some of us hear a "you did a great job" from some grossly less luminary, and our pride heats unharnessed until we nearly self destruct. How much more to hear Paul say that you possess an abundant measure of faith, speech, knowledge, zeal, and love for the messengers of the gospel. At first it may appear that nothing was lacking, but, oh, there was. Paul was well aware that no roster of merits, spiritual or otherwise, could complete the well-rounded Christian without the grace of giving (v. 7).

I never cease to be amazed at those many believers who laud the piety of their lives and the measure of their commitment who are so beggarly in their Christian giving. These same people not only fail to support the budget which they so openly guide to adoption, but they also censor the pastor's messages to challenge the people to know and obey God's will in stewardship. Perhaps this merely refers to the above that there is the barrenness of giving because there is a barrenness of loving.

There comes to my mind an experience related to me by a cousin about a church member we both knew well. The incident occurred perhaps forty-five to fifty years ago.

The church was quarter-time (services were held only one Sunday each month) and had very few financial obligations beyond the limited and ever so inadequate support given to the preacher. There was no water bill—they drank from a spring. There was no gas bill—they heated with wood; and the electricity bill was the minimum REA (Rural Electrification Association) $1.50 for the low-wattage bulbs in the meeting room. And the monthly giving of the gentleman to whom I refer probably did not reach and surely did not exceed fifty cents. Yet the cousin shared the story of the gentleman's riding with him to the little city about twenty miles away and how he consumed the entirety of the trip criticizing the church and pastor for the endless emphasis on "MONEY, MONEY, MONEY."

His criticism was no doubt uncalled for, but it took on real theological significance when they reached their destination. There the gentleman coaxed the cousin off to the side, called him by name and said, "If you'll find us a fifth of whiskey, I'll pay for it, and we'll drink it."

His criticism of God's work was so untamed and unrestricted even though he had probably given less than fifty cents a month. Yet, he was ready, even without being requested, to pay many times that much to purchase alcoholic beverages. Why? You know the answer. It was because the alcoholic drink was the object of his love.

Oh, the barrenness of so many believers in the area of Christian stewardship and how negligent are the shepherds who unfortunately feel that the teaching of stewardship is beyond the realm of their pastoral discipleship responsibilities! Not Paul. In his commitment to develop fruit-bearing Christians, it is no marvel that he wrote to these Corinthians, "see that you also excel in this grace of giving" (v. 7). There is no maturity without it.

Because of the Example of Christ

The believer should give because of the example of Jesus. "For ye know the grace of our Lord Jesus Christ, that, though he was rich, yet for your sakes he became poor, that ye through his poverty might be rich" (v. 9).

On the same basis Paul exhorted the Ephesians:

Be ye therefore followers of God as dear children; And walk in love, as Christ also hath loved us, and hath given himself for us an offering and a sacrifice to God for a sweetsmelling savour (Eph. 5:1-2, KJV).

It is not uncommon for us as believers to speak to one another about the example of Christ in our giving and perhaps even praise ourselves for having followed his example. But I fear that a more careful examination of the 2 Corinthians passage will reveal a level of commitment not usually practiced by any of us. He did not simply give, he impoverished himself. He moved from riches to poverty so he might accomplish his mission.

But let us break down the verse into four singularly distinctive thoughts, even at the possible charge of being homiletical. *First,* there is the prominence of his position – he was rich. This is the point from which he moved to accomplish redemption. And even though the word used here by Paul is somewhat common in describing the prosperity of man, such an interpretation could never fully convey the message of Paul to the Corinthians. They could never hear his word "rich" and liken it to any people among them or to any whom they knew. Their limited measurements were based on material things which they could see and touch and, when bartered, could provide things pleasant, tasteful, comfortable, attractive, sensual, and which could provide security for life. Even though Christ had at His command all of these things, His riches went far beyond the scope of material things.

But how can mortal man describe the riches which Jesus gave up? How can he describe the fellowship of Jesus with the Father? How can he describe the glory of God's throne which surely must have made Solomon's throne look like the phoniness of a beggar? How can he describe the attendance of the multitude of angels when all he has seen are a few incompetent and possibly surly servants who attend the throne of an earthly monarch? How can he even pretend to describe God's table, God's travel, or God's communication in light of what man knows of remotely similar areas of an earthly setting?

Surely he had command of all the wealth of the world, which would boggle the human mind, but He also possessed that abundance which was too secretive or sacred to be described by mere humans. And that, Paul emphasized, was what Jesus gave up for us.

Second, there is that motive of his mission — your sakes. Herein is further described that singularly significant dimension of stewardship: it must be purposeful. The amount of the gift does not define or qualify Christian stewardship. One could give large sums of money for many causes and be a failure in Christian stewardship.

It should be remembered that Jesus did not fall victim to the Roman soldiers who thereafter were credited with His crucifixion. You will recall instead that Jesus reminded Peter that He could have called twelve legions of angels to defend Him if He had wanted to. Twelve legions would have been 72,000 angels, no small group by count. But when one remembers that one angel destroyed 185,000 of the Assyrian army, and so far as we know it was not even a contest, pray tell, what would be the combatant force of 72,000 angels?

I think the passage is noting that He was not taken, and He could not be taken and forcefully crucified by the enemy. Jesus purposed to die. He purposed to fulfill the Father's will. He purposed to pay the supreme price for fallen mankind whom He loved. Jesus gave for a purpose. He impoverished Himself for a purpose. He showed that real stewardship was not victimized loss but purposeful giving. Jesus did it for "your sakes."

Maybe this helps us to see why Paul cited Jesus as the example in proper stewardship. He not only gave so much, He gave it with a noble purpose. Dare we then say to stress verse 9 that giving only becomes biblical stewardship as it is designed to be redemptive? Granted, stewardship embraces how one makes his money, as well as the way it is spent. But is the dimension of Christian giving to be considered as Christian stewardship unless it is ultimately redemptive?

Third, there is the depth of His condescension—"became poor." And there He becomes the unreached goal and example for every believer. Many have possessed some wealth and have given a part of it, but none has given all his wealth as did Jesus. Jesus impoverished Himself. The word "poor" is one connoting "poverty," "beggary," "destitute of riches."

It is not difficult to find noble people who have given abundantly to help churches, missions, students, and other godly causes. But rarely, if ever, would one be found to move from abundant riches to abject poverty to make such gifts. No wonder Jesus was Paul's example of Christian stewardship. He possessed; He gave with purpose; He gave with total selflessness.

Fourth, there is the reward of His giving—"that you might be rich." And even though the word describing "rich" is the same basic word as that used to describe material wealth elsewhere in the New Testament, surely it must be used here to call us back to the earlier part of the same verse in which Paul describes the wealth of Jesus. Indeed, when one accepts the gift of salvation in Jesus Christ, it encourages those qualities of honesty, work, and thrift that contribute to financial wealth. Surely Paul is not claiming that the purpose of Jesus' gift, His death, was to make financial fat cats out of society. Refer back to the all-too-inadequate description of the wealth which Jesus left, and maybe therein one will unearth the wealth Jesus brings the sinner in his salvation experience, an experience that was begun but not yet completed in Jesus.

So, when Paul encouraged the believers to give, he reminded them of Jesus, who gave the paramount gift, and He gave it with a view toward redemption.

To Fulfill Commitments

The believer should give to fulfill any earlier commitments which may have been made. One should not fail to honor his word. "Now I want you to go on and finish it: be as eager to complete the scheme as you were to adopt it, and give according to your means" (v. 11, NEB).

Several months earlier they had been eagerly responsive to the pleas to help the poor saints at Jerusalem, but the cooling of emotions had frozen shut their purses. Time had become the thief of commitment. The winds of spiritual encouragement had subsided, and the tide of unselfishness had washed back into a pool of apathy and selfishness. Now Paul was reminding them that, as believers, they needed to complete what they had promised to do. To me Paul was saying there is a matter of integrity with the believer that if one promises to give, then he should reflect integrity in his giving. But before one becomes disturbed and responds that he made a commitment, and has had financial reverses and should not be condemned for what he cannot do, let him read again the last of the verse, ". . .and give according to your means." Paul does not censure their failure to give what they did not have. Rather, he censured their apathy that forgot their commitment. He criticized the priorities that had shifted from devotion to selfishness.

To Achieve Equality

The believer should give because, with the right attitude, each can have an equal part, regardless of the level of his ability. "For if the willingness is there, the gift is acceptable according to what one has, not according to what one does not have" (v. 12, NIV).

As simple as this may seem at first, one cannot fully comprehend it until he understands that giving is not to help God and keep Him from failing. Instead, giving is a privilege afforded to us. And since it is a privilege afforded to us, one's giving is not evaluated by how much it helps God. It is evaluated by how it relates to the giver. If giving were to be an act of how much God receives based on His need, then the big givers would stand taller because God would receive more from them. But giving is not according to God's need. Blessings for giving are not according to how much God receives to help Him out of difficulties. I repeat, God does not need our money.

Paul pointed out in his sermon on Mars Hill that God is not worshiped with man's hands as though He needed anything (see Acts 17:25). The word here for worship is not one that indicates "praise" and "adoration." Instead, it is a concept of "service." Note the expression, "Neither is worshiped with men's hands, as though he needed anything." This is a picture of one serving another or doing for another what he cannot do for himself.

An illustration would be that of a barber going to the hospital to shave a sick friend. Normally, the patient would have been perfectly capable of caring for himself, but his illness left him dependent and in need. So, the barber went to the hospital to do for the man what he was unable to do for himself. Note again Paul's words that we do not do for God what He is unable to do for Himself. He needs no material gift that we could bring Him.

Therefore, giving is not to help God but to help man. Paul reminded the Philippians, "Not because I desire a gift: but I desire fruit that may abound to your account" (Phil. 4:17). Man must give to develop that spirit of love and Christian unselfishness. One who does not give loses his missionary spirit and grows calloused, selfish, and greedy. And in verse 12, Paul reminds his readers of a glorious and refreshing truth that, if the believer has the spirit of giving, the blessing comes from being faithful in what one has — and that alone. Therefore, one's giving should never be a source of embarrassment but of godly pleasure because, therein, the small giver is just as great as the big giver. Let it be observed, however, that this is no license for small giving by more capable people. It is a cause for rejoicing for all faithful givers.

Because of Integrity in Accounting

Paul challenged these people to give because there was integrity in accounting.

> And we are sending along with him the brother who is praised by all the churches for his service to the gospel. What is more, he was chosen by the churches to accompany us as we carry the offering, which we administer in order to honor the Lord himself and to show our eagerness to help. We want to avoid any criticism of the way we administer this liberal gift. For we are taking pains to do what is right, not only in the eyes of the Lord but also in the eyes of man (vv. 18-21, NIV).

I have no idea if there was a reluctance to trust preachers with the treasury or if Paul was simply taking precautions in a most sensitive and dangerous area. Even as today the people knew then that it was tempting and common for people to dip into the treasury for personal interest without safeguards in accounting. Paul apparently felt he had no right to challenge the people to give sacrificially of their means if he could not assure them that the money would be used for the original purpose for which it was being given.

It is worthy of note that Paul had no subtle intent to "lift" a portion of the receipts for himself. In spite of the absolute integrity intended on his part, he still realized that he had to reckon with any possible suspicions on the part of the people. His commitment to a proper handling of the funds was not enough. He was aware that the people must themselves be satisfied that the funds were handled properly. To do this, a highly reputable layman was enlisted to oversee the handling of the funds.

It was highly in order that Paul call upon the people to give and give freely for the needs of others yet, it also was very much in order that he protect his integrity and assure the confidence of the people in the passing of the money from the givers to the objects of their liberality. It is no less essential today if confidence is to be maintained, and Christian giving is to grow unhindered.

To Be an Example to Others

The believer should give because others need his example. "Therefore show these men the proof of your love and the reason for our pride in you, so that the churches can see it" (v. 24, NIV).

Unfortunately, there is a misguided pseudo-piety among many that prides itself in secrecy in Christian giving. Indeed, there should never be boastfulness of one's giving because one has only what was first given to him. Such Pharisaism was roundly denounced in the Scriptures, but evidently that was not what Paul spoke of because he encouraged the people to give so others might see that expression of their love. You see, God uses the obedience of one as an example to others. That is a well-known method of God.

For example, if one would journey to the foreign mission field and interview the missionaries, it is doubtful if he would find a single missionary who was there because and only because of a Divine revelation of such a call apart from any other influence. Instead, most likely he would hear missionaries tell of when they heard another missionary speak of his commitment to the mission field and how God used that testimony to impress his own heart. We are all impressed spiritually and otherwise by the example of others.

Paul realized the importance of the example of others, and for that reason cited the liberality of the Macedonians when he wrote to encourage the Corinthians to give. As he did he had no reservations about challenging the Corinthians to give that they, in turn, might be an example to others.

In fact, Paul had already used the example of the Corinthians to others.

For I know your eagerness to help. And I have been boasting about it to the Macedonians, telling them that since last year, you in Achaia were ready to give; and your enthusiasm has stirred most of them to action (2 Cor. 9:2, NIV).

As an Expression of God's Grace

The believer should give because it allows an expression for the grace of God. Seven times Paul used "grace" in chapters 8 and 9, but probably none is more cogent than this:

Because of the service by which you have proved yourselves, men will praise God for the obedience that accompanies your confession of the gospel of Christ, and for your generosity in sharing with them and with everyone else. And in their prayers for you their hearts will go out to you, because of the surpassing grace God has given to you (2 Cor. 9:13-14, NIV).

By the giving of the Corinthians, the needy who had received their largess would see their receipts as a gift of God's grace and would praise God abundantly.

It should not be forgotten that we are the instruments through whom God works to supply the needs of others. Indeed, He has no hands but our hands and no feet but our feet. If the hungry need to be fed, God does not drop a bundle from heaven. He uses people to provide for them. If the missionary prays for God's grace to meet a need, God doesn't send money from heaven on angel's wings. He sends it by a believer who thereby is privileged of God.

The cycle is: God gives to us that we may give to others that they may glorify the Lord. The believer's giving is an expression of God's grace to meet a need and when that need is met, God receives glory back from the receiver. And perhaps it should be pointed out that, as one gives as directed by God, He will bless and restock the supply, often many times over, so the steward may have in hand to give again.

Surely God does not give to us that we may amass a fortune for the moth and rust to destroy it or so we may be the object of the interest of the thief. Instead, God enriches His children that they may enrich His work and thereby He may enrich them again.

–3–

Giving Is a Many -Splendored Thing
Basic Acknowledgments of the Giver

Paul's view of the believer and stewardship was centered in the basic acknowledgments of the believer. The very concept of the steward, one who is responsible for the goods of another, causes the Christian steward to make certain basic acknowledgments in his relationship to his Lord. The first of these has been discussed already but is restated here merely to put these basic acknowledgments into perspective, and each will be treated with extreme brevity.

There Is Divine Purpose

The first of these is the acknowledgment that there is a Divine purpose in the believer's life. Without this acknowledgment, it seems that there could evolve complete frustration. How could Paul possibly have commanded the Thessalonians, "In everything give thanks," if there were no Divine purpose for one's life?

Granted, the believer, by foolish choices, can plunge himself into unfortunate and improper circumstances. But, if one's life is confidently led by the Spirit of God, he can rest in the confidence that this is the will and purpose of God and considerably reduce the frustration level. Without it, the believer is constantly found saying, "Why is this happening to me?" "Why am I here?" "Why does someone else seem to get the places of honor and prestige?"

The minister of the gospel must constantly remind himself of the above truth that God has a purpose in what the minister is doing. And if this truly is where God wants him to be, then he has no cause to fret, and worry, and wonder why he is not elsewhere.

When I was doing graduate studies at the seminary I spent an unbelievable amount of time working at a study carrel on the second floor of the library. One day a friend remarked that he did not understand how I could spend those hours there confined at that desk. I was able to answer that I was perfectly content to do that since I had settled in my mind before I ever enrolled that it was God's will for me to do it. There was, therefore, no argumentation or self-pity because as a steward, I was responsible to be faithful or be a rebel.

For every believer, there is that same accountability to know and to do the wishes of the Heavenly Father. He is to be faithful or be a rebel, and to be faithful is both to please the Father and ensure peace and contentment for the believer. The servant has no cause to worry, fret or kick against any restraints if he is doing the will of the Father.

In Paul's writings, he referred to this in at least two ways, both of which have been dealt with earlier and are mentioned again here merely to put this part into perspective. In Philippians 3:12, he expressed the desire to "apprehend" or "lay hands on" that thing that God had in mind for him when God first apprehended him. That seemed to be the consuming desire of Paul as a steward. He wanted to be sure that he knew all along what God had in mind for him to do and having determined that purpose, then he wanted to pursue it with all his heart.

It is reasonable to believe that God does not save a sinner and fail to find something for him to do. God is not so poorly organized and God does not have to secure the weather forecast before planning the day's activities. God has a purpose, immediate and long-range, for every believer, and the believer's greatest privilege and responsibility is to determine God's purpose or plan for his life, and then with serenity, pursue it with all dedication and purpose. Thereby, the Father is pleased, the believer is happy, the Father can bless and the believer is productive and effective.

Paul further deals with this in the passage mentioned earlier from Ephesians 2:21-22, how the parts of the building of God are fitly framed together to provide for the habitation of God through the Spirit.

But he carries this further in 4:11-16, where he speaks of the believer's ministering to the believer, each under the Lordship of Jesus. Here he teaches that the body is built up by the strength supplied by each part as they are supporting one another. Note:

> . . .speaking the truth in love, we will in all things grow up unto him who is the Head, that is, Christ. From him the whole body, joined and held together by every supporting ligament, grows and builds itself up in love, as each part does its work (Eph. 4:15-16, NIV).

Unlike the cancer that erodes and ultimately destroys both the body and itself, the believer gives and ultimately builds both the body and himself.

The believer accepts the place God gives him in the body. — The believer functions in the body in peace and fruitfulness. The head can effectively direct the body's activities, and each part is healthy as each part performs its designated function.

The believer, to be effective, must accept the following facts:

1. God has a plan for his life, immediate and long range.

2. His plan is for the ultimate good of both the individual part and the body as a whole.

3. The believer can find his greatest happiness and effectiveness in the center of the Father's will and purpose.

4. God can spend His time (if I may use these words) "blessing" the believer instead of correcting the believer. Having accepted these positions, the believer has begun his journey toward being an effective steward.

Having accepted the fact that the Father has a plan and purpose for his life, the believer then must confront the truth that:

There Are Multiple Dimensions of Stewardship

Stewardship is multifaceted. In order for the head to effectively use each part of the body, the entirety of that part must be under his direction. The steward is not really under the Lordship of Jesus if part of his life is withheld from that Lordship. He can't give God the days and keep the nights or give God the money (coined life) and keep the God-given abilities. One cannot be effective without the other. To give one part and keep another is mockery. No carpenter can fitly frame together a house if one end of the wood cooperates and the other rebels. No motorist can continue effectively down the highway unless each wheel rolls as he directs it. No artist can communicate his purpose on the canvas if there is rebellion among the colors. And no body can do even the small chores of the day unless each part of the body is responsive to the directives of the head.

It follows, therefore, that for the believer to be a faithful steward, every dimension of this life must be responsible to Divine Lordship.

One such possession mentioned by Paul is "time"—but it is more than *chronos*, it is *kairos*. It is not so many minutes of time space—it is a special time adapted to a certain thing. It is a season or opportunity. So Paul was advising the Ephesians that they would be wise if they made use of every opportunity, "making the most of every opportunity" (Eph. 5:16, NIV).

To me, this is awesome. To be a faithful steward, one must not let pass by unpurchased one single special opportunity that God has given. He should never stand at the counter trying to decide whether or not to take it. He should "buy out" every special opportunity given by God. And when he considers that opportunities bought bring even greater opportunities, and opportunities neglected will find them offered to another, it is enough to cause one to cry, "help me to be a faithful steward."

A similar exhortation is made in Colossians where Paul challenges, "Make the most of every opportunity" (Col. 4:5, NIV).

So the faithful steward is one whose life is effectively controlled by the Lord. If events, times, and opportunities are all bought out, it would mean that at moments when one is tempted to slander another, instead he will bless. When the decision about education and training could become a sellout for a life of secondary effectiveness, the steward buys the opportunity and sharpens his skills for effective ministry. When the moment of moral temptation would bid for a sellout, the steward instead does a buyout. When the moment for altering the records, and a sellout would wreck one's integrity, it becomes instead a buyout, and a steward's life is healthy and vibrant.

Second, one is advised that he is a steward of his body. This was Paul's personal desire. Immediately before this, "For me to live is Christ" (Phil, 1:21, KJV), his words were, "so that now as always Christ will be exalted in my body, whether by life or by death" (Phil, 1:20, NIV). Paul rejoiced in the prayers of the Philippians on his behalf, and he earnestly expected to be freed. But whether set free or killed, he desired and was cognizant that Christ would be exalted in his body.

Perhaps one might contend that Paul was simply saying, "God's will be done; let it be life or let it be death." I do not doubt that calm resolution was there, but surely it was more than a passive commitment. It was an active pursuit. Surely, if they took his body in death it would be giving to God that which was His already. But if he lived, it would be a body held in trust from God and over which he would preside as a resident caretaker. No sinful poison would flow in its veins. There would be no sedate functionary systems that deteriorate for lack of exercise caused by simple lethargy. There would be no tissue that is chalky and passive because of years of nicotine's progression in making them little more than death. There would be no failing heart that has labored with the overload of obesity. No! If Paul would be spared the executioner, his body would reflect that superior maintenance peculiar to the believer who is a faithful steward.

One of the clearest expressions of Paul on the body is found in these words:

> I beseech you therefore, brethren by the mercies of God, that ye present your bodies a living sacrifice, holy, acceptable unto God, which is your reasonable service (Rom. 12:1, KJV).

In Paul's expression here he clearly ran counter to the belief of the Greeks of his day who believed that the body was only evil, and no good could come from it. Greek philosophy and religion adhered to the concept that the body was only the prison in which the spirit of man dwelt and which would be freed when the body died.

That was not Paul's message to the believers. Their bodies were a stewardship accountability to God. The body was to be used for worship unto God. That body may be digging in the mines, driving a truck, preparing a meal, or designing a building. Whatever the task laid upon it, the body should do its work as "spiritual worship" (Rom. 12:2, NIV). Therein, the believer, as a steward, is declaring to God, "All I am is yours, and it is dedicated to your glory."

Third, Paul speaks of the stewardship of the mind, and he begins by giving some negative advice. Don't use your minds the way the pagans use theirs, he said. "So I tell you this, and insist on it in the Lord, that you must no longer live as the Gentiles do, in the futility of their thinking" (Eph. 4:17, NIV). The Ephesians at one time had lived in that very same manner when they were unbelievers. They had thought as the "pagans with their good-for-nothing notions" (Eph. 4:17, NEB). Their whole thought process was an exercise in futility. "Vanity" is the word used by the *King James Version*. Their thoughts were for security when there was no security; their thoughts were of gods that were only idols and destined to destruction; for pleasure which invariably ended instead with pain; of vengeance that led to more hatred; of self that led to more greed and egotism; of the freshness of temptation that led to animalistic wretchedness. And to these Ephesians, Paul was urging, don't do as you once did. Harness the mind and will to do those things for your physical and spiritual good and for God's glory. Ride herd on your mind. Be a good steward of that which so acutely affects all of life.

Something of the same thing is found in his comments in the Book of Romans, "Do not conform any longer to the pattern of this world, but be transformed by the renewing of your mind" (Rom. 12:2, NIV).

There are two Greek words for "new" in the New Testament. One is "new" with reference to *time*, and the other is "new" with reference to *kind*. The latter is found in verse 2 and Paul therein cautions his readers against following a pattern of life directed by a mind like an unregenerated mind. Instead, their lives were to be under the direction of a mind being transformed by the Holy Spirit – a new kind of life directed by a new kind of mind.

So the stewardship accountability becomes quite clear. The words and the deeds emanate from a mind that is dominated by either the flesh or the Spirit. The steward can feed his mind on trash and vulgarity, and his life will become dominated by the same. Or he can feed his mind on pure, wholesome, and spiritual things, and his life will be shaped accordingly.

This renewing process, according to Paul, is to enable the believer to prove (not to test the trustworthiness but to prove to himself its validity) the good, acceptable and perfect will of God (see Rom.12:2). In the constant renewal of the mind in the Holy Spirit, the steward finds the will of God for his life. And how absolutely imperative it is for the steward to learn the will of his Master if he pleases Him in his responsibilities. Only therein could he possibly honor the exhortation of Paul found elsewhere:

> I appeal to you, brothers, in the name of our Lord Jesus Christ, that all of you agree with one another so that there may be no divisions among you and that you may be perfectly united in mind and thought (1 Cor. 1:10, NIV).

Suffice it to say in concluding this part that all instructions of Paul to the believer in any area become a stewardship accountability for which each is to be faithful. This would be true concerning the gospel (Acts 20:24-31), wives to husbands (Eph. 5:22-24), husbands to wives (Eph. 5:25-29), children to parents (Eph. 6:1-3), parents to children (Eph. 6:4), servants to masters (Eph. 6:5-8), and masters to servants (Eph. 6:9).

There Are Gifts in Giving

It should also be observed that believers have gifts in giving. The gift of giving is like all other gifts of the Spirit. It grows in effectiveness with use, and as other gifts of the Spirit, it is best enjoyed when clearly identified.

Perhaps there are several ways to identify the gifts of the Spirit in one's life such as the apparent presence of the phenomenon and the latent joy that follows its practice. However, the gift of giving surely must birth in the experience of spiritual commitment to Jesus. There is not real commitment until the totality of one's life is turned over to Him. The experience may be traumatic and it may require a lot of soul searching, but one can never practice that gift of giving so long as he regards the priority of self.

The problem is, any thought of giving provokes a deep-seated debate to determine whether the gift should be given or whether it should be used to purchase something desired for one's self. So long as this is taking place, Jesus is not on the throne in our lives. But when He is enthroned in our lives, then it is easy to take what we have in our hands, and bringing it to Jesus say, "You first."

And when that occurs, there is the desire to give. With the desire to give comes the opportunity to give, and with the opportunity to give come the resources to give, and with the resources to give comes the joy of giving, and with the joy of giving comes the blessing for giving. Thus, the cycle keeps repeating itself, and with each repetition there is expansion. But with expansion does not come the normal, attendant selfishness. Instead, it continues in an ongoing pattern of exercising one's gift whereby God is glorified, and the believer is blessed.

Paul's words to those who possessed that gift of giving were: "if it is contributing to the needs of others, let him give generously" (Rom. 12:8, NIV). This latter part is translated by the *New English Bible*, "give with all your heart," and Phillips renders it, "give freely"

Here some simple observations are in order:

1. A gift is that which one receives from another. The gift of giving is a gift from God.

2. Precious gifts should be treated with reverence.

3. Gifts should be exercised according to the purpose of their design. A highly bred racing horse should not be carelessly allowed to stand daily in the confines of a small stable.

4. Gifts are enhanced with use. The gift of an expensive automobile deteriorates if left to stand unused.

5. An unused gift dishonors the one who gave it.

6. The giver will give again if the receiver accepts the gift with thanksgiving and enhances it by use.

7. In the example of spiritual gifts, one's gift is for the good of the body and never for selfish ends (see 1 Corinthians 12:27-28;

Eph. 4:7-16). The purposes of my heart and my liver are different, but my body is healthy as each performs the task it was gifted to achieve.

8. Gifts are enjoyed when not compared to the gifts of others or when we do not envy the gifts of others.

9. A gift can never be bought. The moment a price is paid, it ceases to be a gift. And if it is purchased it brings on negotiation, debate, assessment of value and joy, or regret in the transaction, and none of these can appropriately characterize the gift that we received of God. It should be accepted with thanksgiving, used to fulfill its purpose, and enjoyed for the peace it gives.

The gift should never be exercised beggarly. Giving is a privilege and should be expressed "generously," "with all your heart," and "freely."

The Believer Is Wealthy

The *fourth* and final acknowledgment of the steward is that the believer is wealthy. Oh, I do not mean that every believer possesses an abundance of cash or stocks or real estate. There are people with those possessions who feel very poor in the things that really count. I grow a bit weary hearing Christians lamenting their lot in life and denigrating the economic level of other believers. They do not have anything and perhaps never will. They never expect any better and would be shocked if things did get better. They are still committed to the concept of those who contend that if it is good-tasting or physically pleasant, then it is evil.

So one believes that he must accept the worst of everything in life if he would be "spiritually committed," and I fear that the result is a self imposed and highly unpleasant deprivation which makes the person miserable, a hypocrite for claiming that he is not, and little honor is brought to God.

In 1 Timothy, Paul addresses the matter of the believer's attitude toward wealth, and we shall deal with that later. Suffice it to say that he does not denounce the presence of wealth but the emotional and selfish attachment to it. He cautions against certain problems of wealth and tells them how to use it for their own benefit and enjoyment.

Surely no one would really object to the claim that the believer is wealthy, and Paul speaks to that in 1 Corinthians where he first denounces the pursuit of worldly wisdom and the division it produced in the church. One of the problems he found in the Corinthian church was their choosing sides as to whom they would follow, and with each choice there was an attendant attitude of superiority. But Paul said to them:

> So never make mere men a cause for pride. For though everything belongs to you — Paul, Apollos, and Cephas, the world, life, and death, the present and the future, all of them belong to you — yet you belong to Christ and Christ to God (1 Cor. 3:21-23, NIV).

It seems evident that Paul was trying to make a point by strong contrast. In his effort to crumble the egotism which grew out of a claim that one belonged to Paul or Apollos or Cephas, Paul spoke by contrast, "They belong to you. You have the benefit of the ministries of all these men. You are wealthy," And when I recount how my own life has been blessed by the ministry of several great men of God, I realize indeed how rich I am.

But is that all Paul communicates in this passage? I think not, for he spells out other things after saying, "everything belongs to you." He does name the three great preachers, but he also mentioned (would you believe it?) the "world," and that is not the sinful world system but the ordered structure about us. What does Paul mean with "the world is yours?" No doubt he is pointing out that the things of the world do not have you but *you have them*. They do not have control of your life; you have control of them. You do not earn income in order to bail out from a slavery brought on by greed for things. You are able to use possessions as you please to the glory of Christ.

Paul also must be teaching that the things of this world are at our disposal. Why should we have no resources with which to feed our families? Why should we have a mission program with no resources to carry the gospel? Why should we have no place of worship because there is no money to buy land or materials? Why should God's work grind to a halt or exist on charitable tips handed off by those who would mock as quickly as they would give support? You perhaps sound off, "It isn't fair!" I agree, and I add, "It isn't necessary." God is quite able to supply the needs of His work if His people would only believe that He is able and trust Him for the results.

I propose to deal only with the writings of Paul but let me also cite Hebrews 3:19, which may be his, in which the writer recalls to his readers the failure of the people of Israel to enter into the promised land: "So we see that they could not enter in because of unbelief" (KJV).

Paul also states that "life" is theirs. Of course, they did not have the power to give life. But in a very real sense, their lives belonged to them. They had the privilege of using their lives as they wished. Concerning his own life Paul said, ". . . and the life which I now life in the flesh I live by the faith of the Son of God. . ." (Gal. 2:20, KJV). As one who belongs to Christ (1 Cor. 3:23), the believer has a hold on life that is a life worth living. And, as Paul further states in this passage, he has a hold on Him who makes death glorious and not fearful.

In deference to brevity, let me observe that Paul continues his emphases with the same expanded thought that both the present and the future also belong to the believer.

Perhaps we should now leave the subject of wealth and the believer and venture no further subjective comments, but allow me to comment a bit on this subject that often draws rather heated discussion.

First, let me point out that God is not poor. I often think of what must be the appearance of God's throne. I will not presume to describe it, but I cannot perceive of it as being constructed of poor materials in need of painting and surrounded by wind-blown candy wrappers or stained with smudgy finger prints. Not God's throne!

Of course, the Son of Man while here had no place to lay his head, but was it because he could provide no place to lay his head? Of course not. Instead, Jesus set the example for all of His followers to accommodate the gospel to the needs it was to fulfill. That is exactly what Paul did throughout his ministry and precisely what we should be willing to do.

In my college days, I was disturbed about a young man who purposely projected an image of poverty. His clothing and his conduct reflected it. For several years, I wondered if I lacked spiritual commitment by wearing the best suit I could afford. Was I really as humble as I should be and would God be honored more if I were to reflect poverty?

So, I settled that matter in prayer, and it has not bothered me since. I promised the Lord that I would be pleased to wear rags and choose the other accouterments of my life accordingly if that was what He wanted and what would honor Him. I not only said it, but I meant it. I wanted my life to honor God whatever that may have required of me relative to possessions. At the same time, I became convinced that there was no honor brought to God in self-inflicted poverty. If I were diminished to poverty while striving to achieve the best I could, then praise be to God for it!

Yet, I concluded that, first of all, I would earn what I could in a manner that would be honoring to God and not as a result of greed. I would never neglect His work, and I would never *seek* the place where I might serve. I have never requested to be called to any church nor have I asked to be recommended to any work. Too, I would always be sure that a tithe of all I made went to God with opportunity for additional offerings as He led. Next, I would provide for my family and myself the best quality of life's needs I could buy.

Long ago I concluded that the lowest-priced items may, in truth, cost the most. So, buying was done with care and discretion. If we bought clothes or furniture for the home, we have used them all with a sense of pride and thanksgiving to God, and we have been perfectly willing to give it back to Him if He should ask for it.

He is the Lord of the universe, and I feel He is to be the Lord of my life. If that means giving up everything and living in poverty, then may I have grace to obey His will. Still, if He does not ask it, why should I presume to exhibit my alleged devotion with a poverty that, deep-down, I perhaps disdain?

Somehow I feel that showing off is unbecoming to the child of God and should be shunned as a disease — but quality, cleanliness, attractiveness, worn or used, without any degree of vanity, demonstrativeness, or egotism helps set apart the believer as a child of the King and a servant of the Lord.

Although this is not designed to include the other inspired writers, I will briefly deal with 3 John 2, in which a desire is expressed for his reader, Gaius, to prosper; but one should look at the context. Gaius evidently used the bulk of his resources to provide food, lodging, clothes, and other provisions as was needed by the itinerant preachers who enjoyed his hospitality. To him, John simply referred, (and I paraphrase), "Gaius, for one who uses his wealth to bless the cause of Jesus, I pray that God will give you more and more."

Indeed I could sincerely pray the same prayer for the man or woman today who takes the resources given by God and keeps on using them to spread the gospel. For you, my dear friend, since you use what God gives you for His glory, I pray that you may prosper more and more!

After this review of the "the acknowledgments of the steward," more than likely, the next logical discussion would be Paul's claim that:

The Steward Is Accountable.

The very nature of stewardship demands that special emphasis be given to accountability. If stewardship is the disposition by one of the goods of another, then accountability is at the heart of stewardship. A good or bad steward largely can be determined by the response to accountability. At this point the believer takes his stewardship seriously, and the paramount level of accountability to Paul was that:

The steward is to be faithful. – "Moreover it is required in stewards that a man be found faithful" (1 Cor. 4:2, KJV). This may, at first, seem to be lightened responsibility, but is it? A more careful look at the verse will reveal a rather awesome picture. The word "faithful" seems simple enough, and perhaps it is, but it is more than a plain exercising of faith; it is an expression of loyalty. "Faithfulness" is that response of one who faithfully carries out or fulfills the orders, commands, or the wishes of another. In this example, it would be the believer who fulfills every wish and command of the Master. So, let your mind reflect for a moment on the awesomeness of fulfilling every wish and command of God in His Word.

The word "steward" used here means the management of a household or the manager of the household affairs of another. It is the picture of a servant who had been given the heavy responsibility of total supervision of the wealthy landholder's estate. He is a steward.

"Required" seems to be clear enough, but it conveys more than what first might be observed. It is not a legalistic binding. Instead, it comes from the word "seek," which seems to imply that "it is sought or required."

So, one can observe in verse 2, that the one thing God looks for and longs to find in those intrusted with the management of His estate is: that he be a person who will, without argument, carry out God's every wish and command. What a view of stewardship! What a comprehensive emphasis! It doesn't bother to deal with money, time, talent, the gospel or anything else. Here, Paul gave his sweeping and emphatic view of stewardship—God will require of the one to be trusted with His earthly estate that he be unashamedly obedient.

Perhaps it would be appropriate to link with this emphasis on obedience, Paul's promise of rewards. Truly this is a New Testament dimension of stewardship and should not be viewed with apology or disdain. Just as certain as Paul exhorts to unequivocal obedience, he also promises unmistakable rewards. To the Ephesians he wrote, "You may be sure that God will reward a man for good work, irrespective of whether the man be slave or free" (Eph. 6:8, Phillips). To the Galatians he affirmed, "Let us not become weary in doing good, for at the proper time we will reap a harvest if we do not give up" (Gal. 6:9, NIV).

Not only is the steward required to be faithful in the management of God's estate, but he is accountable for the way he acquires his wealth. It should be earned. —The believer should never hold in his hand the wealth he acquired by selling drugs or alcohol that could and often do destroy the lives of others. He should not possess wealth that was obtained by improper rental receipts from those who were unable to counter his unreasonable assessments. He should never boast of money that came from inordinate profits on misrepresented and inferior goods.

God had spoken to His people by Moses that in their dealings with others they should not steal, deal falsely, or lie to one another (see Lev. 19:11). If such restrictions were honored today, I fear that a large portion of sales, either in goods or services, would be wiped out. Note the three areas of restraint: (1) Don't take the goods, the services, the clients, the property, or the good name that belongs to someone else. It is stealing. (2) Don't negotiate any trade with a man that would cause him later to say he had been duped. (3) Don't deal falsely in your word given to another. Be as good as your word. God's people were always supposed to deal honestly in their relation to their fellow man. Such honest accountability reflected a right relationship of the steward to his God. This was exactly what Paul was emphasizing in his letter to the Romans when he cautioned, "Recompense to no man evil for evil. Provide things honest in the sight of all men" (Rom. 12:17).

The Master does not put into the hands of his stewards monies he took from another of his own, and the steward had best not scheme and plan to accomplish it on his own. The steward should constantly ask himself if he has in his hands that which was received in any way other than a fair return on goods sold and services rendered, or that which was received as a gift from another.

Paul felt strongly about this. In fact, even though he taught that the laborer is worthy of his hire, he provided for himself by his own labors, so no one would presume to indict him for ill-gotten gain.

> After this, Paul left Athens and went to Corinth. There he met a Jew named Aquilla, a native of Pontus, who had recently come from Italy with his wife Priscilla, because Claudius had ordered all the Jews to leave Rome. Paul went to see them, and because he was a tentmaker as they were, he stayed and worked with them (Acts 18:1-3, NIV).

As a rabbi who appropriately had learned a trade as rabbis normally would do, Paul sought an opportunity to pursue that trade and provide honest earnings for himself without the necessity for his support resting on the shoulders of his new converts. Such also allowed Paul to stay close to the working men to whom he would minister.

This has become extremely difficult in our commercialized society. How can the minister rub elbows with his working people? But even though it is difficult, the preacher must not lose touch with the burdens of the working man or woman, or he would lose sight of realities that would color or shape his ministries to these people. He must never lose touch with the headaches, backaches, and heartaches of his people if he would know how to minister to their needs.

But labor for wages to Paul was more than earning sufficient monies to meet one's needs. It was also to provide monies that could be used to give to the needs of others. This would then grow out of a proper mental attitude on giving. "In everything I did, I showed you that by this kind of hard work we must help the weak, remembering the words of the Lord Jesus: 'It is more blessed to give than to receive' " (Acts 20:35, NIV). You see, part of the motivation for earning is the privilege to give, and the motivation for giving is a transformed attitude of the mind. Part of the reason for work is to be able to give; the motivation for that kind of remarkable attitude on giving is a thinking that one had rather give to someone in need than to wait for someone to give to him.

The actual meaning of this verse is more than that. The word for "receive" is not the meaning conveyed in the word "accept" as to accept something given by one to another. Instead, it is a word which conveys the meaning "to take" or "to grasp for oneself." So it is more than pleasantly accepting what is given by another. It means aggressively to seek to acquire for oneself.

So Paul declared to these Ephesian elders, and to us, that we should work and acquire wages for our labors with a mind-set toward what we can do for others and not with a mind toward grabbing more goods for ourselves. How far we have moved away from this attitude in today's society! How bent we are toward acquiring more and more for the gratification of the flesh, and subsequently we wonder why the world does not do more for us. How blessed it would be if, with gratitude for the many blessings of God on our lives, we would labor further to acquire what we may be able to give to another.

Paul conveys this same meaning to the Ephesians, only in this Epistle he gives an additional emphasis by stating, "He who has been stealing must steal no longer, but must work, doing something useful with his own hands, that he may have something to share with those in need" (Eph. 4:28, NIV). A similar idea is set forth here, except Paul carries the "receiving" one step further. Here "receiving" becomes "theft," and that should come as no great surprise. If one does not have the mind to give but instead has the mind to "receive" or to "reach out to grasp for oneself," the very next step is to feel that the world owes one what he seeks to have for himself. Since the world owes it, anyhow, one reaches out to claim it illegally.

Here Paul does not quote Jesus as in Acts 20:35 — that it is more blessed to live a life to give instead of a life to reach out to grasp for oneself. Instead, he now says to those who have "received" that they should now cease, and instead of stealing, they should earn their needs and also earn from their wages so they may have wherewith to share with others. Paul's stewardship emphasis developed a mind that thought of how to give and not how to receive.

Three truths are to be clearly gleaned from this passage:

1. *The error of stealing.* — To steal is to take the life of another, for goods are "coined life." The bills, coins, or checks brought home by the laborer are his life. He has put into that his mind, his body, his time, his emotions — yes, all that he is. He has poured a part of his life into that pay.

2. *It emphasizes the rightness of work.* — Who in his right mind would see dishonor in work. It is healthy; it is honorable; it is rewarding; it is a facet of maturity. Work is that involvement of the otherwise selfish person who now decides he will cease to be a selfish burden on others and instead will provide for himself.

3. *It also emphasizes the believers' care and concern for the needy.* — Work provides an opportunity for one to have in hand that gift God may lead one to give to another, without which he would miss the blessing of being a channel of God's goodness to mankind.

In Paul's Second Epistle to the Thessalonians he also addresses the matter of one's work, not only that one might earn his bread, but also that work is a way to occupy one's time and helps keep one from evil. In this severe denunciation of gossip (2 Thes. 3:11-12, NIV), he suggests that if one's time were spent in productive activity, then he would not have time to meddle into the affairs of others. That is still good counsel!

The believer should pursue his course in the will of God. — Even though I have dealt somewhat with this dimension already, no study on the accountability of the steward would be complete without addressing the will of God for that believer. Without it, stewardship becomes a misnomer. A steward is not a steward without accountability to the will and wishes of the master in whose household he serves. No steward can be called faithful who does not serve in the purpose and plan of God.

So, then, it follows that the steward must accept the fact of God's will, exercise diligence to determine that will, and personally find joy in the pursuit of it.

In the life of Paul, (1) He acknowledged the sufficiency of God's will. It is good (for the needs of people), acceptable (that which is acceptable or pleasing to God), and perfect (complete to cover every dimension of life, Rom. 12:2). (2) With sensitivity he obeyed the will of God (Acts 16:6-10). (3) He found personal satisfaction in the course of his life (Phil. 4:11).

It seems rather easy to write or to read these lines and conclude with a hearty, but entirely too casual, "amen." Herein, though, is the profile of the great steward: he/she sincerely accepts the sufficiency of God's plan for his life, is sensitive and alert to respond to God's plan, and finds personal joy and complete satisfaction in the pursuit of that plan.

I fear that many believers never address their willingness to obey God's will and chafe under conditions that subsequently displease them.

With his full stamp of approval, Paul spoke of Epaphras, who apparently was from Colosse, that "he is always wrestling in prayer for you, that you may stand firm in the will of God, mature and fully assured" (Col. 4:12, NIV).

We should endeavor to grasp and feel the heart of this pastor as he desired for his people to be rightly related in the will of God. No flock could please their minister more than to know and do the will of God. What more could he ask of his congregation? They could not be better stewards than that.

Some significant truths for the steward surface from this passage:

1. *Living in the will of God brings confidence.* — One cannot "stand firm" without the confidence that he is in the will of God, but therein he is bold and fearless.

2. *Living in the will of God brings aggressiveness.* — One is ready to press forward with the knowledge that his course has been directed by the Lord. Paul encountered no small amount of opposition, but he never retreated. Instead, he pressed the charge into the camp of the foe.

3. *Living in the will of God brings maturity.* — God's will is perfect or complete for the life of the believer (Rom. 12:2), and living in that will moves one toward inevitable growth and maturity. Maybe Paul was emphasizing the same truth to the Corinthians when he wrote:

> And we all, with unveiled face, beholding the glory of the Lord, are being changed into his likeness from one degree of glory to another; for this comes from the Lord who is the Spirit (2 Cor. 3:18, RSV).

4. *Living in the will of God brings assurance.* The fact of the will of God for one's life is not enough. There also must be the assurance of the will of God. The believer must do more than talk about the will of God; he must learn the details of God's will for his life.

The example of the slave so perfectly describes the steward and the will of his God. The will of the master dictates the activities of the household or estate. He conveys his wishes to the slave for he expects the servant to hear the expression of his wishes. The master expects the loyalty and obedience of the servant. In return, the good master subsequently meets every need of the servant.

The steward is responsible for the care of his own. — Paul's language, concerning one's care of his family, is a rather strong expression and causes the reader to remember his statement to the Corinthians that, "I am not commanding you" (2 Cor. 8:8, NIV). Perhaps he is not commanding, but it is a rather strong suggestion when he says, "If anyone does not provide for his relatives, and especially for his immediate family, he has denied the faith and is worse than an unbeliever" (1 Tim. 5:8, NIV). Paul knew that the believer was free to make his own choice in the distribution of his financial resources. However, he had no reservations in instructing a young congregation that no genuine believer would think of failing to give for the upkeep of his own family.

Conceivably someone might ask whether financial support of family members is, after all, truly a part of biblical stewardship. The answer, of course, is no — it is not a part of one's tithe to his church; but yes, it is a part of one's stewardship of the resources entrusted into the care of the steward.

Two widely differing opinions prevail among Christians in this matter. First, there are those who believe that the support of the church comes *after* one has provided for the needs of his loved ones. Second, others believe that not even the care of a needy loved one should take away from one's gifts to the church.

I believe that neither position is irrefutably accurate. It is a mistake to give to the needs and wants of a family member to the erroneous neglect of the church. Also, one can give to the church under an assumed banner of piety and easily err in the care of his loved ones.

I wish it were possible to present a biblical formula for the solution of this question. If only the Bible would say that no family need should deter our steadfast giving to the church, or if it would only say that a certain level of family need justifies a redirecting of church gifts to that family need, then we would have our answer – but it doesn't. The text above clearly expresses Paul's wishes that no believer should fail to care for the needs of his family.

Even though I propose in this writing to stay with the teaching of Paul, please allow me to remind you what Jesus taught about using holy goods for the needs of one's life. Recall the time that the disciples, who were with Jesus, were plucking the ears of corn on the sabbath day. Jesus not only justified their doing it, but he cited the example of David who, to meet a need, ate the holy bread which was for the priests only (Mark 2:23-28). Also, reflect on the story of Jesus who denounced the worshiper who designated his goods as "corban," or dedicated to holy use, and thereby avoided sharing it with his needy parents (Mark 7:11).

Let no one leap on this as an excuse for redirecting income from the church to a loved one. I think that seldom, if ever, would one find the choice to be an either/or. But if it should seem to be so, let us remember that the people whom Paul describes as worthy of our support are truly needy and worthy people (1 Tim. 5:3-13).

The steward is responsible for the care of those who live of the Gospel. – Perchance this is the most common or first-accepted dimension of stewardship – "taking care of the preacher." And to discuss this, I want to stress the wording of this heading, "the steward is responsible."

Often the preacher is or has been treated as an object of charity to which perhaps comfortable church members toss a few crumbs of their surplus to help God provide for a hungry preacher. Or there have been junk sales or bazaars, etc. to raise enough money to pay the preacher's salary because church members would not tithe.

By handling it in this manner, the preacher's family is treated as second-rate citizens; the people develop a mentality of "helping God," which casts God in the role of being dependent on humans, the church members grow selfish in feeling that what they have is theirs, and they are not stewards at all. Furthermore, the church members miss the joy of faithful stewardship and sacrificial giving.

I have four basic statements about the support of those who preach the gospel. *First*, it is a biblical principle, "Even so hath the Lord ordained that they which preach the gospel should live of the gospel" (1 Cor. 9:14, KJV). To affirm this, Paul uses four analogies (1 Cor. 9:7,10) and quotes Moses on still another (1 Cor. 9:9). It is compared to a battle where the soldier is supported by the country which sent him out. The soldier does not march with the army three days and provide his livelihood the other four days of the week. No soldier could be at his best if he had to concern himself about his basic provisions.

Then Paul likens it to a man who plants a vineyard and is thereby privileged to eat of the grapes — the results of his labors. Another tends the flock and because his time is committed to the care of the flock, he is to enjoy the provisions therefrom. Later he speaks of the plowman who cultivates the crop and because of this, he expects to share in the harvest. And he cites Moses who says that the ox should not be muzzled when he is treading out the grain. He was to eat of the fruits of his labor. With the same emphasis to Timothy, Paul says, "The husbandman that laboreth must be first partaker of the fruits" (2 Tim. 2:6, KJV).

It seems there really could be little question about the meaning of these and certainly not when Paul, with the statement cited earlier, emphasizes, "Even so hath the Lord ordained that they which preach the gospel should live of the gospel" (1 Cor. 9:14, KJV).

Paul had not exercised this privilege (1 Cor. 9:15), but that fact did not reduce his emphasis to the people that this should be practiced.

Churches who heed this seriously open the pathway for God to bless them in their obedience. How well do I remember when in an early student pastorate, the church made a bold step of faith and increased my salary. I felt that God placed His approval on that act when two young people were saved the following Sunday. Yes, it is an inescapable biblical principle.

Second, it is a Christian obligation. Paul used some very strong language when he addressed the Galatians about their support of their ministers.

> Be not deceived; God is not mocked: for whatsoever a man soweth, that shall he also reap. For he that soweth to his flesh shall of the flesh reap corruption; but he that soweth to the Spirit shall of the Spirit reap life everlasting (Gal. 6:7-8, KJV).

Surely someone will contend, "But that refers to moral conduct. If one sows bad seed, he will reap a bad harvest; if one sows good seed, he will reap a good harvest." Granted, it has often been interpreted that way. But to do so leads to an impossible interpretation of the Scripture, one to which neither of us would be willing to go, namely, that if one does good works, he can gain eternal life apart from the sacrifice of Jesus Christ.

Let's walk through the verse on the premise that it is speaking of moral conduct and let's see where it leads us. Note the first part: "Be not deceived, God is not mocked." No problem there. Surely one should not be deceived into believing that he can conduct his life as he wishes and that God will take no note of it.

The next statement, "for whatsoever a man soweth, that shall he also reap," likewise creates no problem. It is a declaration of fact whether or not referring to moral conduct. Then "he that soweth to his flesh shall of the flesh reap corruption" follows, and there still is no problem. Surely no one questions the verity of one's reaping problems if he sows the seeds of ungodly living.

But now arises the problem, "but he that soweth to the Spirit shall of the Spirit reap life everlasting." If one sows good works — sows to the Spirit — he shall of the Spirit reap life everlasting, or eternal life. The problem is evident, and it clearly reveals an error in interpretation because the Bible does not contradict itself. To claim that one can sow good works and reap everlasting life is blatantly contrary to the remainder of the Bible.

Then what does it teach? It is a lesson on stewardship. The clue to its understanding is found in verse 6, which seldom is seen in its relation to this passage, "Let him that is taught in the word communicate unto him that teacheth in all good things" (Gal. 6:6, KJV). The parts, "him that is taught" and "him that teacheth," clearly identify the parties under consideration. And the one who is taught is to "communicate" to the one who teaches. This word "communicate" is the same as Paul used in his letter to the beloved Philippians when he wrote, "When I departed from Macedonia, no church communicated with me as concerning giving and receiving but ye only" (Phil. 4:15, KJV).

In this Philippian passage, Paul clearly is expressing gratitude to them for sending support to meet his needs. They had "shared" with him; they had "communicated" with him. In verse 16, Paul said, "For even in Thessalonica ye sent once and again unto my necessity."

It also should be added here that immediately after this statement in Philippians, Paul's words reflect his spirit and attitude in his dealing with the people with whom he labored — he wanted them to be fruit-bearing Christians. "Not because I desire a gift: but I desire fruit that may abound to your account" (v. 17, KJV).

So Paul is stressing in Galatians 6:8 that if one spends his money in worldly ways, to the flesh, then he shall in so doing reap a harvest of destruction; while if he chooses to sow or invest it in spiritual things, then he shall of that sowing reap a harvest of souls born into the family of God.

I trust that this illustration may help to interpret it for us. Imagine that I held in my hand a fifty-dollar bill and asked if that bill were morally good or morally evil. One would perhaps answer that the bill was neither good nor bad—that the moral implications would be in the use of the bill by the owner. The bill could, of course, be used for the purchase of good things or bad things, and it would have the same monetary value in each case. It would be of equal value and would be equally as well received in the bar for an alcoholic drink as it would at the church in the offering plate. The same fifty-dollar bill!

So, if it has equal value in either place, if it would be welcomed in either place and the choice of either is in my power, then I must make a decision. Do I sow it to the flesh, or do I sow it to the Spirit? The decision is totally mine. The money is a gift of God, but it is in my custody and I can do with it as I choose. Of course, I am warned in this passage that I cannot thumb my nose at God. I will reap the harvest of my choice, but the choice is in my hand.

For the sake of the illustration, let's assume that I choose to sow to the flesh. I spend that bill and many more like it for, say, many years. I have made my choice, but God has likewise given His warning—I will reap what I sow. I will reap destruction, and reap I do! The years bring their heartaches and grief. Drinking, profanity, cheating, pornography, or any number of other areas of exploitation deliver their bitter end—an incurable drinking problem, a broken home, or a life on skid row. Having sowed to the flesh, I have of that sowing to the flesh reaped destruction.

Likewise, for the sake of the illustration, let's assume that I choose to sow to the Spirit. The decision is mine. The money is in my hand. I have made my choice. Let us imagine that a missionary offering is being received to send a fine young couple to the foreign mission field. As the offering plate is being passed, I weigh the decision to give and decide that I, too, want to have a part in that missionary undertaking. I choose to sow to the Spirit. Surely my giving my fifty-dollar bill to the support of Christian mission work would be sowing to the Spirit. So I give my offering right along with the offerings of others who likewise choose to sow to the Spirit. Together our offerings, and those subsequently given, keep the missionary on the field where an effective work is done for God.

Then one day the missionary family returns home on furlough and the pastor invites the missionary to preach on Sunday morning, but he asks him only to give a report of his missionary work since the people hear the pastor preach every Sunday and because they would want to hear about the mission work. So, on Sunday morning, the missionary shares with the people about the geography of the mission area, the social structure of the people, and then delightfully reports, "And just this year I have led twenty-five souls to Jesus."

If I were seated in the audience, I would remain silent in respect to the occasion, but I would want to stand, interrupt the missionary, and ask, "Who led them to Jesus?" That would, no doubt, frustrate the speaker, but the question would be valid, because all of us who gave to the support of the missionary and sustained his efforts, had a part in his leading the twenty-five souls to Jesus. What has occurred is that I have sowed to the Spirit, and I have of the Spirit literally reaped life everlasting or everlasting life. I have taken money that was at my disposal, I have sowed it to the Spirit, I have given it to the ministry of the Spirit, and I have, from that sowing, reaped the lives of lost people on the mission field. I have reaped life everlasting!

This is a blessed promise to the giver, and I share this encouragement with believers wherever there is an occasion to do so. I remind them that their gifts for the work of God, whether it be the support of the ministry or the erection of a building, are gifts that will ultimately reap the harvest of lost souls for Jesus.

Who can measure the endless chain of harvest that can come from one's sowing to the Spirit? A gift to the erection of a place of worship may seem so very simple. But what of the boy who may be led to Jesus because of that place of worship, who himself may preach the gospel and of whose converts some may go to the mission field. It then becomes an endless chain of harvest. No wonder it has been said that God does not give us our reward when we die. You see, the books are not totaled then. That endless chain of harvest has not been reaped. The unending return on one's gift to the ministry of God's Word has not yet been completed.

No wonder Paul continues by saying, "And let us not be weary in well doing: for in due season we shall reap, if we faint not" (Gal. 6:9, KJV).

Third, it is a promise from God. I enter this only for the sake of emphasis achieved by an outline. For in the treatment of Galatians 6:6-9, I have sought to point out that Paul not only warns against neglecting this responsibility, but he also promises that the harvest will be realized in the reaching of souls or in bringing the lost to life eternal.

It also would be appropriate to remember that when Paul spoke of the support given to him by the Philippians, he reminded them that their giving would abound in fruit to their account (Phil. 4:15-17).

Fourth, it is a joy. Only those who have not experienced it would question the fact of joy in giving. When Paul spoke to the Ephesian elders about his own support of himself to avoid being dependent upon others, he cited the words of Jesus that "It is more blessed to give than to receive" (Acts 20:35, KJV). Granted, he spoke of supporting the weak, but he also had been talking about support of the ministry. So, it is reasonable to assume that he must have likewise intended to say that one who supports the ministry is happier than one who lives only to acquire gain for himself.

The selfish heart has trouble grasping this truth because all financial attention is given to efforts to enrich one's own coffers. Happiness to them is another good investment, another good sale, another big deposit. But this inevitably leads to a dwarfed spirit, a selfish mentality, a fearful outlook. Even couples who have no children must guard against this spirit because the lack of parental financial responsibility often causes one likewise to fail to care for others and become more and more bent on acquiring wealth which may issue in less and less happiness in the doing of it. Nothing cures a selfish heart like a giving hand, and nothing turns unhappiness to joy like fruit in the life of another that has been watered by the unselfish hand of a giver.

Paul likewise knew that our heart follows our treasure and that support of the ministry will contribute immeasurably to the joy and sweet attitude of the giver. People tend to support the ministry in spirit when they support with their money. What a joy to feel that one has had a part in the full-time preaching of the gospel by one's minister for whom one has given his support.

The steward must consider the harvest. — In two great passages Paul uses the scene of the farmer to illustrate his teachings on stewardship. In Galatians 6:7-9, he comes down hard on his readers by using the principle of the harvest to warn them that they will reap what they sow in giving.

The other passage is 2 Cor. 9:6: "He which soweth sparingly shall reap also sparingly, and he which soweth bountifully shall reap also bountifully."

But this passage should not be explored without first looking at the companion verse 7 which reads, "Every man as he purposeth in his heart, so let him give; not grudgingly, or of necessity: for God loveth a cheerful giver." As in verse 6, so also in verse 7, there are the contrasting parties. In verse 6, the contrast is between the one who sows sparingly and the one who sows bountifully. In verse 7, the contrast is between the one who gives grudgingly and the one who gives joyfully.

Surely none would deny the connection between these two verses where the one who gives sparingly is in the camp with the one who gives grudgingly, and the one who gives bountifully is compared to the one who gives joyfully. The pairs cannot be separated. The grudging or sour and reluctant heart will not freely distribute that which he clings to so dearly. He would always give or sow sparingly, while the cheerful or "hilarious" giver will freely or bountifully sow or give to the glory of God. In fact, the word translated "bountiful" in the KJV carries the idea of celebration with praise.

It seems ironic that we would give so sparingly to the cause of Christ in view of this promise of the harvest. The God of the harvest has clearly promised that we shall reap in direct proportion to our sowing, and still we gather such a limited harvest. Is it because of the lack of faith? Are we afraid that if we give we will thereby deprive ourselves of needed material possessions because when we give it is gone? Is this the problem? Do we lack faith? Then we are to be ashamed. God has never broken a promise. God wants us to trust Him, and it must be an insult to Him when He promised us a bountiful harvest and then we argue, "But God, I'm afraid You may not do it." That is an insult. Do we really fail to sow because we lack faith?

Or maybe we fail to sow because it looks too much like waste. After all, our gift (the grain) is perfectly good grain and to throw it broadcast on the loose soil is too much like throwing it away — like waste. It may appear to be wasteful if we lose sight of God. In a literal sense, I see that grain as thrown away if I lose sight of the warm, fertile soil on which it has fallen, the power of generation of that seed, and the dynamics of remarkable multiplication in that plant. Hopefully, each single grain of corn will sprout, grow, and put on ears of corn; with each stalk bearing two ears, and each ear bearing approximately 1,200 grains, the one grain has multiplied to 2,400 grains. But this will never occur if I view sowing as throwing away the seed.

Or do we fail to sow because we have so little grain and, really, all of it is needed for food? I think this is often the situation, but it holds the potential for a tragedy if one consumes the grain and has no seed to plant.

I do not question the need for eating all of the grain, and many feel they cannot give because they need all they have to live on. If one does that, then there will be no harvest because there has been no planting. Isn't it better to prepare for a harvest? Why not consider the supply of grain (one's income) and determine to use part of it for seed? One should take the choicest, though the amount is small, lay it aside for God, and discipline oneself to live on the remainder. Then in the harvest, there is more than ever before. Thus, more can be dedicated for seed the next year, and thereafter will follow the larger harvest. Soon one is able to plant big fields and reap big harvests. I believe it would contribute to clarity and inspiration if this should all be put in perspective with a brief outline on the harvest.

First, God gives the seed. There is no way that humans can make a seed. Science has advanced to remarkable levels, but no laboratory has yet produced a seed. Only God can put into a little case the potential of life found in a seed. Likewise, it should be remembered that only God can give us "the power to get wealth."

Second, God gives the field. How often it has been appropriately observed, "They aren't making any more ground." Only God can give the soil in which all seeds are planted. Likewise, God will provide the field in which to give our possessions. We should not take this lightly. The seed should not be carelessly thrown out onto rocky ground. One should find the warm, fertile soil where the seed will sprout and grow.

Third, God gives the increase. The farmer cannot grow one single seed into a plant. He can guard the seed, handle the seed, or talk to the seed, but he will never give it life. Only God can do that.

Fourth, people must plant the seed. God can make the seed and provide the soil but man must plant the crop. This is so important. A person should unselfishly choose the best grain that he has for seed; he must choose the best possible soil for planting; then he must surrender the seed. Having done so, he should water and cultivate in faith, remembering that only God can give the increase.

I would not want to draw from this passage that which Paul did not intend to teach, and I do not wish to stretch the metaphor beyond the simple truth that Paul wanted to communicate, namely, if one wants a big harvest, he will need to plant a big crop.

However, there might be a truth in saying this: not only does God give to us the seed for planting, but He only measures to us the seed to plant He considers that we are capable of cultivating. Such would be compatible with similar truth taught elsewhere.

In any event, I shall conclude this portion with three simple but pungent truths about sowing and reaping: One always reaps what he sows; he always reaps more than he sows; he always reaps later than he sows.

−4−

A Room Full of Mirrors
Attitudes of the Steward

Proper stewardship is not only a matter of the investment and distribution of the goods of another, it also involves the attitude of the steward in the achievement of these matters. As in other dimensions of life, it is not merely the doing of a task but one's attitude or disposition while doing it. Sometimes parents are heard to remark, "I would rather do it myself than to hear him grumble and complain while doing it." On the other hand, management in some companies speak of their employees in such warm words of commendation, "Not only do they do good work, but they have such a wonderful attitude about it."

Paul likewise wrote copiously about the attitude of believers toward their stewardship responsibilities.

Greed and Arrogance

First, Paul sorely denounced an attitude of greed or ostentation. Greed loses sight of the amount and perhaps the sufficiency of that which one already has and, thereby, obliterates the gratitude for what God has already done. The greedy person always sees what he currently has as inadequate, inappropriate, or unworthy and, therefore, without his heartfelt appreciation.

Greed always stresses the worthiness of the possessor, that he "deserves" what he has. Therefore, it is inevitable that one feels he deserves more than he has. It also follows that one compares his possessions with others which also prompts the greed for more. And, of course, there follows the likely failure to share what one has as God would lead him to share. So the progression in improper attitude for the believer is (1) self-sufficiency, (2) merit, (3) comparison, (4) selfishness, (5) greed and (6) ingratitude. This is a rather ugly list of characteristics, and all of it grows out of or leads to the attitude of greed.

On the qualifications of bishops, Paul writes that he should be "not greedy of filthy lucre" (1 Tim. 3:3, KJV), or "No lover of money" (NEB). And of the deacon he says, "Not greedy of filthy lucre" (1 Tim. 3:8, KJV), or "Not...given...to money-grubbing" (NEB). See also Titus 1:7.

The word used to translate the first of these (1 Tim. 3:3) would lead us to believe from the KJV that we should abstain from an eager, intensive, and unreasonable pursuit of more money. Yet, the other dimension of greed enters here with pungency and emphasizes that one should not only refrain from ungodly pursuit, but also should avoid a selfish and covetous handling of one's possessions. Once again, it is from the spirit of selfishness that the spirit of ungodly ambition is born.

In the second example (1 Tim. 3:8), warning is given against ill-gotten gain. The prefix in this original word turns "gain" into "base gain" or "filthy lucre." The same prefix, when used in reference to "speech," turns that into "low and obscene speech."

This should be no surprise, though, because one's attitude of self-sufficiency, leading to his feeling of personal merit, his comparison of his state with others, and the resultant selfishness and greed, all lead inevitability to one's pursuing that wealth by less than honorable means.

Allow me to lament that so many people have allowed their greedy pursuit of money to lead them at last to practices that were immoral, often illegal, and sometimes self-destructive.

The above area that Paul condemns, one's greed for money growing out of a spirit of selfishness and comparison to others, is followed now with the apparel of women which, too, is rooted in that attitude of selfishness, greed, vanity, ostentation, and comparison, only this time the party is trying to outshine others who also may be attending the worship of God (1 Tim. 2:9-10). And it is all a matter of the attitudes of the believer, attitudes which are so much alike that there would be some difficulty in separating them. The desire to excel others which leads to greed is the same desire to excel others that would lead to the wearing of ostentatious apparel.

I don't think that it rightly can be assumed for a moment that Paul is advising the believer that the only acceptable dress is drab, rough or unkempt clothes. That could attract more attention than the finer pieces. Indeed one could bring reproach upon his or her position with ragged and cheap clothes. Paul surely is condemning an attitude of vanity that would cause a woman to adorn herself in gold or pearls that would indicate an attitude of superiority and arrogance.

In the worship of God, the rich and the poor should be able to sit side by side without either being critical of the other. The rich person should not look with disdain on the poor woman who has come with a pure heart and wearing the best she can afford. Neither should the poor scorn the rich whose normal attire is the discriminating clothing peculiar to their possessions in life.

So often the wealthy are singled out for their criticism of the poor, but the poor can be equally as guilty of unjust verbal abuse of the wealthy. It is all a matter of attitude of the believer. Is she dressing "up" or "down" so as to call attention to herself? If so, selfishness, greed, and ostentation have supplanted a meek and quiet spirit of that believer who should desire, above all else, to honor Him whose Name is worthy.

Let it likewise be remembered that Paul would not let the people give him financial support lest they would claim he had preached for gain. An ungodly pursuit of wealth which expressed itself in greed and showiness was, in Paul's life and teaching, an improper attitude for the Christian steward.

Giving is a matter of the heart, not only of the purse. Early on, the good steward must learn that the responsibility for faithful stewardship is not fulfilled in simply giving an amount of money. Stewardship to Paul, and should be to the believer today, is also a disposition of the heart.

Pride

One's giving should be without pride. "Do nothing out of selfish ambition or vain conceit" (Phil. 2:3, NIV).

> Your attitude should be the same as that of Christ Jesus: Who, being in the very nature God, did not consider equality with God something to be grasped, but made himself nothing, taking the very nature of a servant, being made in human likeness. And being found in appearance as a man, he humbled himself and became obedient to death — even death on the cross! (Phil. 2:5-8, NIV).

So often the believer finds himself making such statements as "I earned it," "It's mine," "I deserve it," "I'm worthy," all of which fly in the face of the precious words in which Paul reminds us that Jesus was indeed equal with God but that did not stand in the way of His fulfilling His mission to redeem mankind. Instead of pride and arrogance, He made himself nothing; He became a servant; He became like unto fallen man, yet without sin, that he might pay the price and redeem the lost.

None of us can do what Jesus did, even if it remained yet to be done, which it does not, but there is a task that every believer is called to accomplish. It may be small, or it may be large. It may cost little, or it may cost much. It may require a small portion of what one has, or it may require all that one has. But the question arises, is one willing to lay aside whatever is dear to him for that which is dearer to God? The steward should be without ungodly pride.

Willingness

One should give with freedom of the will. Some may at first wish to question the statement that it is not the money but the attitude that counts, but it must be that way. If it were the money that counted, then God would weigh our faithfulness by how much money we gave. To make that conclusion is to claim that God is dependent on us and that He needs the money we give. This would be indicating that God is not really God, but that He is dependent upon man. This is not true, of course, for God is more than adequate. God is not dependent on us. God does not need the money we would give. Instead, He wants our devotion. He wants what we want to give to Him.

A biblical example might help to clarify this. In the story of the fall of man it is recorded that God placed in the Garden of Eden "the tree of the knowledge of good and evil" and made it "off limits" for Adam and Eve. This may seem strange to the casual reader who wonders why God would place the tree there and make it "off limits" for them. If He did not want them to eat of it, why did He place it there? If God really loved them, why was the temptation there for them to sin? And the answer is found in observing the one response that God wanted from man then, now, and always, and that is *his love*. But, you see, love cannot be proved without choice. Devotion by coercion is not necessarily affection.

For the sake of clarification, let us imagine that God had placed Adam and Eve in the Garden of Eden and had told them He wanted only their love, and He gave them no opportunity for choice or rejection. God could have dictated, "I am the object of the total affection of My creation." But could He really? When there was nothing they could do but show God devotion, could it really be called love? No! Persons must have the choice. Man must, of his own free will, choose to give his devotion to God. God's love to man was not and could not be shown in keeping man from sin. God's love has been expressed to man in offering him redemption from sin even after man chose not to love God.

People have always been able to exercise their free will, and Paul so clearly expresses that in his teaching on stewardship. To the Corinthians he instructed, "Each man should give what he has decided in his heart to give" (2 Cor. 9:7, NIV). This is the only acceptable way to make an offering unto God.

In his encouragement to the Corinthians to complete their offering commitment, Paul stopped short of a commandment but suggested instead, "For if the willingness is there, the gift is acceptable according to what one has, not according to what he does not have" (2 Cor. 8:12, NIV).

This matter is perhaps nowhere more vividly expressed by Paul than when he wrote from the prison cell to his friend Philemon about the conversion of Philemon's former slave, Onesimus. Paul wanted to keep Onesimus so he could minister to his need — "so that he could take your place in helping me while I am in chains for the gospel" (Phile. 14, NIV).

Onesimus had run away from his master, Philemon, and had found Paul, whom he had apparently known from Paul's earlier visits to the house of Philemon. While visiting with Paul in his prison cell, Onesimus heard the witness of Paul and was saved. Even though Paul loved Onesimus and wanted to keep him in Rome, he sent him back to Philemon to whom he spoke these moving words, "But I did not want to do anything without your consent, so that any favor you do will be spontaneous and not forced" (Phile. 14, NIV).

Paul wanted any gift from his friend Philemon to be exactly what God wants in our gifts to Him, a voluntary or free-will expression of our devotion.

Regret

Giving should be without regret. In 2 Corinthians 9:7, the *King James Version* translates, "Every man as he purposeth in his heart, so let him give; *not grudgingly*" (author's italics).This really is not a bad translation. These words mean "not from grief," or "not to sorrow or grieve for something." One should never give to God with a feeling of sorrow, grief, or regret. Such an offering ceases to have meaning for the giver. God receives from us what we want to give to Him, not what we let go with grief and regret.

No wonder the offering of the Macedonians was so meaningful to Paul because "they urgently pleaded with us for the privilege of sharing in this service to the saints" (2 Cor. 8:4, NIV).

In a Capital Stewardship Program I conducted in Marietta, Georgia, a young man expressed his intent to give $10,000 to $12,000. At that point he would have been very reluctant to give more because he had in mind other things he wanted to claim for himself. Any larger gift would likely have been given from grief or regret. However, this young man and his wife spent much time in prayer, and he returned the next day to report that they were committing $250,000 to be given over a three-year period. This was indeed exciting news, but his follow-up statement made it even more meaningful when he exclaimed, "And I have the greatest feeling of contentment I have ever had in my life." He was giving without regret.

Compulsion

Giving should be without compulsion. Again, 2 Corinthians 9:7 reads, "Each man should give what he has decided in his heart to give, not reluctantly *or under compulsion*" (author's italics). The believer should never give and feel that he has been taken advantage of. His giving should never be because he is forced by others but because he wants to give.

It is hoped that this point has not been stressed to excess, but the believer must give out of his own choice and not from coercion. And interestingly enough, when one gives because of coercion it often takes the form of an obligation "to support God who needs it very badly." It is almost as though God were dependent on our gift and unless we give, God may go out of business.

At times I have the feeling that we believe God is following the ushers down the aisles of the church, looking over their shoulders as the offering is given to see if enough is being received to keep Him solvent. But let us remember that if God is dependent on our gifts to keep Him solvent, then He fails to be an all-sufficient God and instead, is dependent on our frailty to sustain Him.

God may, indeed, look over the shoulders of the ushers as the offering is being received, but it would be to observe our faithfulness, which He can bless, and not our sharing to keep Him solvent.

Another form of compulsion common today is a mail request that makes one feel that if he does not rally to the request that he will miss a genuine blessing that could otherwise be provided only by the sender's intercession or design. I personally resent that kind of pressure and somehow feel that they are intentionally trying to make me give in a manner that Paul specifically forbids — by compulsion.

Cheerfulness

Giving should be done cheerfully. Really, this is the antithesis of what has gone before — not from grief and not under compulsion but cheerfully. If one regrets his giving, gives from grief, or gives under pressure from someone else, he certainly cannot be giving cheerfully.

No doubt most readers of Christian books are already aware of the Greek word which here is translated "cheerful" ("hilarious" actually from *hilaros*). But Paul's using this word as he does, surfaces a meaningful dimension of the word.

So often we cite the Greek words *hilaros* or *hilaron* as used here and dismiss it simply by stating that God wants a "happy" giver. True, He does want happy givers, but Paul arrives at the greater meaning of this by contrasts. That is, God does not want a gift that is given with regret or out of grief, and God does not want a gift that is made under compulsion. Note that both of these apparently grow out of an external influence or force.

God does not want us to give with regret, which is what happens when we give under compulsion. Instead, God loves a cheerful giver, and a gift given cheerfully seems to be more than a gift of hilarity or fun, but is a gift of generosity, freely given from the heart of gratitude for what God has given to a person. This word is not used to describe God who gave but *man who gave*. God's gift was what He alone and no other could give. Man's gift is sharing what God has first given him. The joy of man's gift is not just because he can give, but *because he will give*. So Paul makes it plain that God wants givers who are really saying, "I want to do this, and I would not have it any other way."

When a person vows he won't give, he has grown another layer of callousness over his heart with the resultant cynicism, criticism, fear, distrust, and somberness. When a person decides he will give from the heart, he has stripped away another layer of callousness and has allowed the freshness of the Holy Spirit to breathe upon his soul. And whether or not there is open exhilaration, there is a joy like that of a boy when he has given up all his little comforts for himself in order to buy one special gift for his dad. In quiet exultation he thinks, "I would not take it back for the world" — no regret and no compulsion, just pure joy. Maybe that illustration can help to explain "for God loves a cheerful giver"; and perhaps that passage will also help us to understand why there is never an expression of regret in all the writings of Paul.

—5—

A Word to the Wealthy is Wise
A Look at Wealth

Years ago I heard what was perhaps a fictitious story of a wealthy man who requested to be buried in his gold Cadillac by which, even in his death, he would display his opulence. So, on the day of his burial, he was placed in his gold Cadillac and as a crane gently lowered the car containing the body of the deceased into a huge grave, one small boy said to his friend as they observed from a mound of dirt nearby. "Man, that's living."

Such a response was no doubt what the man had wanted to elicit from those who observed. But the truth is, the man had gone out into eternity and none of the apparent affluence had been able to follow him.

An Example

It is appropriate to look first of all at one who was a believer and known to be wealthy. The story is found in Acts 16:13-15, NIV.

On the Sabbath we went outside the city gate to the river, where we expected to find a place of prayer. We sat down and began to speak to the women who had gathered there. One of those listening was a woman named Lydia, a dealer in purple cloth from the city of Thyatira, who was a worshiper of God. The Lord opened her heart to respond to Paul's message. When she and the members of her household were baptized, she invited us to her home. "If you consider me a believer in the Lord," she said, "come and stay at my house." And she persuaded us.

Some facts about this first Christian convert in Europe are left to conjecture. However, it is reasonable to assume that she was a widow. She was wealthy and a worshiper of the true God. She trusted Jesus in saving faith. She was instrumental in the salvation of others in her house and she extended the comforts of her home to Paul's missionary party.

From these apparent truths, there are some valid conclusions to draw about the proper attitude toward wealth:

1. No amount of material things of this world is able to give peace to a troubled heart.

2. One left with absolute control of wealth should not use it to the neglect of the worship of God.

3. Wealth should not be a substitute for one's faith commitment to Jesus.

4. Wealth should not be a hindrance to one's being a personal witness to others about Jesus.

5. Wealth should be used to extend hospitality and assistance to those who bear the Gospel to the unsaved.

Lydia's wealth may have come to her from her deceased husband, or it may have been the result of the enterprising undertakings made by an industrious lady after being widowed. In any event, she was a dealer in purple cloth, a product so rare and expensive that it would have required a tremendous wealth to have functioned in such a capacity.

Since there was no synagogue in Philippi, Lydia and others who worshiped the true God, gathered at a predetermined place near the river where on the sabbath day they could worship God. Paul and his companions apparently had heard about the place for it was, "where we expected to find a place of prayer" (v. 13). The occasion afforded Paul an opportunity to teach those who gathered and as a result of the fruitful work of the Word and the Spirit, Lydia responded in faith and became a believer in the Lord Jesus Christ.

Apparently she encouraged others of her children or of her servants who made up her household likewise to respond and they, too, became Christians. Thereafter, that lovely Christian virtue of hospitality came into focus as she urged Paul and his party to remain in her home while in the area. This they did and later when Paul commended the Philippians for their thoughtfulness (Phil. 4:15), he must have remembered that it began in the example of a lovely and wealthy lady who had become a follower of Jesus.

So, from this passage, Paul would have us learn certain foundational truths about wealth (see p. 70): (1) that it should not stand in the way of one's believing in Jesus; and (2) that it should be a means of assisting those who preach the Gospel.

A Spiritual Gift

One who has the gift of giving, should do it with simplicity. To the Romans, Paul says, ". . .he that giveth, let him do it with simplicity. . ." (Rom. 12:8, KJV). The NIV translates this "generously," but I fear that "generously" could lead one to a false concept of what Paul is intending. For example, a wealthy person could read the word as "generously" and interpret Paul's message as being that one who gives abundantly has met the pattern of giving for the believer. Therein is a fault that is constantly feared and fought by pastors today whose members want to give their liberal checks to the church and having done so, excuse themselves from all subsequent personal responsibility.

Paul is not simply implying here that one's responsibility as a giver is to give generously. Instead, he teaches that if one would be a giver, he should do so with simplicity, singleness of heart, mental honesty, and oneness of mind in Christ. Paul seems to be teaching the giver that he give with oneness of purpose, and mere obedience to the Holy Spirit, just to honor the name of Jesus. The contrast here is that Paul again is condemning giving that has as its purpose the gaining of personal recognition or personal benefits for the giver.

Warnings

The believer is warned against purposing or willing to be rich (1 Tim. 6:6-11). Plenty in this passage is written about an attitude toward wealth and to achieve a measure of clarity, I shall continue with a rather strict outline of the material.

The real goal to be achieved is "contentment" (v. 6). — This is reserved for a later segment called "The Goal of the Steward." But suffice it to be said here that this word for "contentment" is found elsewhere in 2 Corinthians 9:8, where it is translated "sufficiency," meaning one needing no aid. Just the thought of that is exciting but we shall discuss it later.

The second emphasis in this passage by Paul is that one cannot take it with him (v. 7). — It appears to be such a transparent truth, but how soon we forget and pursue wealth as though it were an eternal commodity.

Perhaps it would be a good reminder to all who strive for personal gain to go by the hospital nursery where, except for perhaps a diaper, they can see how much they can really take out with them.

One should be content with the basics. — "And having food and raiment let us be therewith content" (1 Tim. 6:8, KJV). We need to remember that when we feel we deserve more, we tend to lack gratitude for what we have. Greed and gratitude cannot find lodging in the same heart. Here this truth helps us to understand what Paul is writing, "Coming in you had nothing (zero) and going out you will have nothing (zero)." Now in verse 8, he says that, since you started this life with nothing and you will end it with nothing, you have cause for gratitude, even when God provided only the basics. You came in naked—He will provide raiment. You came in hungry— He will provide food. Therefore, having these, be satisfied and grateful to Him to whom we owe our gratitude for all our blessings.

The next emphasis of Paul in verse 9 should be prefaced with some observations.

Some may see this statement as being out of place and feel it should come at the beginning of this passage for, indeed, the emphasis here does form the basis for the entire passage. That is why I have chosen to designate this entire portion as warnings against purposing or willing to be rich. That thought is taken from verse 9. But the verse does not belong earlier. Instead, Paul gives positive but general statements which could stand alone as one positive message (vv. 6-8), but they also form the basis for more personal and direct applications and exhortations. I agree that "But" in verse 9 is not adversative in which would be implied the thought "but—however—instead." Paul really is saying, "and having food and raiment, let us therewith be content because those who will to be rich incur many problems." Paul seems to be emphasizing his encouragement to the people to find satisfaction with food and clothing, the basics, because those who purpose to acquire an abundance above the basic food and raiment are risking many possible problems.

One should avoid perilous dangers (1 Tim. 6:9).—It should be understood candidly that Paul does not equate these problems with wealth as such. Instead, he equates them with the person who *wills* to be rich, the one who purposes and pursues a determined goal to achieve riches. Such a mental attitude, such a disregard for the feelings of others, such a willingness to set aside principles of moral integrity, such a relentless pursuit of money, will inevitably result in these problems he names and problems he advises the believer to avoid.

1. *The danger of falling into temptations.* The verb "falling" implies a ceaseless recurrence of this falling into or toppling back over into temptations. If one should intently pursue the acquiring of wealth, there will be the inevitable "need" to resort to ungodly means to achieve such wealth. It may be to cover up book entries in order to achieve more for oneself. It may be to market an ungodly commodity because there is an easy sale for the product. It may be to take away the fair ownership of a partner in order to possess all or most of the company for oneself. It may be to engage in questionable moral conduct which is perceived to be the way to achieve the wealth one desires and purposes to achieve.

2. *The danger of falling into a snare.* Having succumbed to temptation, there is the subsequent likelihood of falling into a snare or trap whose gaping jaws wait to close in on whoever carelessly comes that way. As a bird delightfully eats the grain appropriately set to catch him, he is not aware of the quick response of the snare or trap until he is caught fast in the jaws of it. Alcoholics, prison inmates, or saddened divorcees never knew that these actions would be the end result of the temptations to which they responded in their relentless pursuit of wealth.

3. *The danger of falling into many foolish and hurtful lusts.* Here Paul speaks of the subsequent and ensuing desires as being foolish. Many vain or foolish desires seem to be inevitable if one should intently pursue wealth.

One such desire of him who would pursue wealth is the desire for security. He thinks that if he can successfully acquire wealth, then there will follow the inevitable security. How foolish. The truth is, many who achieved wealth have found feelings of fear and insecurity never known before with less financial responsibility.

Another desire is for contentment. But actually, with wealth there is the constant fear of losing it through improper usage or by someone's forcefully taking it away.

Others desire satisfaction and feel that when their goal of wealth has been reached, they will have enough. Not so. Instead, the heart that wills to be rich keeps wanting more and more. There is never quite enough. Therefore, satisfaction is an illusive dream still being sought without peace until death calls it all to a halt.

Some desire or lust for the power that comes with wealth, but power is that which exalts self and often results in a ruthless disregard for the feelings of others. Power can accomplish good for others. Yet, it designs hurt for others because social integrity would preclude the amassing of wealth which the greedy heart has sought, and often one is saddened by the hurt and isolation he has brought to others.

Still another has willed to be rich because of a desire to find honor among his fellow men. But, alas, he finds that honor has eluded him and, instead, he is disliked and distrusted by those from whom honor would have come.

4. *The danger of a ceaseless sinking or drowning.* — There is something terribly final about "sinking to the bottom" or "drowning" as the *King James Version* has it. Earlier in verse 9, Paul speaks of one's being caught in a snare, and here he refers to sinking to the bottom. Is he merely returning to repeat the same thing for a second time? I think not. In the first example he speaks of the snare that waits to entrap those who recklessly pursue wealth, but he leaves open the possibility of escape, as slim as the possibility might be. Here he speaks of those who keep on pursuing foolish and hurtful desires until at last one sinks to the bottom or drowns in destruction or ruin.

But the words "sinking" or "drowning" are not poorly chosen when one examines the word for "perdition" or "ruin" at the end of this verse. For one cannot escape the meaning of final and total destruction. In fact, the meaning is that of final destruction brought on by one's own self. How sad to think of those who have relentlessly pursued wealth to gain all those things thought to characterize wealth, only to find that they have missed "the pearl of great price" and, too, have been responsible for obstructing the way of others who otherwise might have been saved.

Then, after Paul, in verses 6 through 8, has admonished his readers to be content with the basics, and in verse 9 has warned them against the willful pursuit of wealth, now he comes in verse 10 to speak of the fact that:

There are sad results of such a monetary pursuit. Paul stated these results as follows:

1. *They have erred from the faith.* — The vast possibilities of wrong latent in money are expressed by Paul as he observed that the love of it "is the root of all evil," and that some who followed that love had wandered away from their commitment to Christ. Such pursuit has often led to the tenuous joys of recreational houses and equipment which, instead of strengthening their commitment to Christ by their devotion in gratitude, have caused them to leave the house of God and find pleasure in the possessions their wealth has bought.

The pastor who notices the prosperity of his members wants to rejoice in the blessings of God on their lives, but instead of their prosperity bringing devotion and gratitude to God, he often sees them forget the hand of God's goodness, and they fulfill instead the desires for the pleasures their money can afford. Paul recognized this as a grave problem for the believer.

2. *"They have pierced themselves with many sorrows."* — The sad part about this statement is that it speaks of self-inflicted destruction. It seems strange that people would intentionally stick pins into their flesh to suffer the consequences of such pain, but some have done exactly that. One who relentlessly pursues the acquiring of wealth will cause one "sorrow arrow" after another to be shot into his heart. How many have sought the presumed blessings of wealth only to find instead one sorrow and heartache after another. Instead of joy, there is heartbreak. Instead of satisfac-

tion, there is insatiable desire. Instead of security, there is fear. Instead of friends, there are often those who just lie in wait for one's departure so that they can pounce on one's money. Instead of treasure in heaven, there is only earthly store that soon will be left behind. And the tragic thought is, a greedy person has brought it upon himself. He has pierced himself with many sorrows.

The understood cause must be observed. It would be well here, at least for outline's sake, to return to the 1 Timothy 6 passage and list the causes for these ultimate problems. They are lucidly delineated in verses 9 and 10.

1. *There is the will to be rich (v. 9).* — One's relentless search for wealth, with the disregard for more noble pursuits, will ultimately reach the unhappy end that is mentioned above.

2. *Then there is the love of money (v. 10).* — Please note that the passage is appropriately translated, "the love of money." These are not words and deeds of impersonal or casual interest. It is literally an "affection" for money that immediately puts it on a collision course with other concerns that merit one's love and often are sacrificed to satisfy the utter love of money.

3. *It was coveted after (v. 10).* — The word used here for "covet" means "to long for intently," which is not too unlike the two words used earlier which were to "love" money and to "will" or purpose to be rich — but there is a significant distinction. To "covet" is to want it badly. To "love" it is to bear a burning affection for it. To "will" for it is a deliberate purposing in one's heart to achieve it. Perhaps in reverse order, these are the actual steps in the fatal error of the believer. First, he mentally considers it or wants it. Second, his heart embraces it with affection and desire. Third, he wills or purposes in his heart to achieve it.

Contrasts

Next comes the contrasting commitment for the believer. In verse 11, Paul admonishes the believer, "But you, man of God, flee from all of this, and pursue righteousness, godliness, faith, love, endurance and gentleness" (NIV). Paul pled with the believer to flee the dangers he named as one would run from a storm or a beast or a serpent. He is not to run a distance and presume to rest in safety. There is no final safety in distance. He is never to cease fleeing but to keep on fleeing.

Positive Graces

Then Paul follows the negative with the positive, and just as the positive is opposite the negative, these likewise are opposites of those against which he warned above. As one is to go on running from the above, he is to "follow after" or run swiftly and with intensity in pursuit of these six positive graces.

1. *Righteousness* — that conduct of persons God would call "right." Our money-crazed society has, unfortunately, lost sight of this one.

2. *Godliness* — that speaks of one's spiritual devotion to God.

3. *Faith* — This had to appear as a contrast to the negatives above because the opposite of one's selfish pursuit for himself is his simple dependence on the providence of God. Recall without my comment the story of Jesus about the birds of the air and the lilies of the field. Recollect also the story from 1 Kings 17 about God's provision for Elijah when He had commanded the ravens to feed the prophet.

4. *Love* — How little can one write about love? Perhaps it would suffice to observe that this is given in stark contrast to one who loves wealth and wills to secure it, even if it means hurt to others.

5. *Patience or endurance* — Patience is not described by one who idly sits with folded arms while the world goes by. Instead, patience is that spirit of endurance that sticks to the task and refuses to give up. It is the spirit of the believer who views the apparent financial prosperity of others and is offered an opportunity to sell out his commitment and join the ranks of those who

are "at ease in Zion" or who have erred from the faith, but instead he sticks to his commitment and refuses to give up or to sell out.

6. *Meekness or gentleness of spirit.* — Once again, this is set in contrast to the spirit of ruthlessness that would trample on the feelings and possessions of others to achieve one's goal of wealth.

These are those qualities the believer should pursue, and they are set in contrast to those influences from which he should flee as from a charging beast.

Helps

Paul's instructions to the rich are helps for the wealthy believer.

It should be clearly observed that, despite the earlier pleas, Paul does not condemn wealth. He was fully aware there were dangers in having wealth which many people could not handle. But he did not condemn wealth. Paul knew that some then possessed wealth, and that others would later acquire it. Thus he undertakes to list some guidelines for these people as enumerated in the following verses:

> Command those who are rich in this present world not to be arrogant nor to put their hope in wealth, which is so uncertain, but to put their hope in God, who richly provides us with everything for our enjoyment. Command them to do good, to be rich in good deeds, and to be generous and willing to share. In this way they will lay up treasure for themselves as a firm foundation for the coming age, so that they may take hold of the life that is truly life (1 Tim. 6:17-19, NIV).

Wealthy believers should avoid the paramount temptation of pride: "be not highminded" or "not to be arrogant." — The possession of wealth no doubt constitutes a blessing for those who are rich, and although the wealth may be received by perfectly legitimate means, there are certain dangers even for the believer to avoid. The first of these dangers is pride. There is a constant peril of the wealthy person's feeling he is better than those who are poor. Perhaps one would hastily affirm that he would never think that he was any better than anyone else, but wouldn't he? What if his luxury car was parked beside a poor man's more utilitarian vehicle? What if their grocery baskets sat side by side at the checkout counter? What if seats were to be chosen for an athletic competition? What if they conversed of vacation trips with half a globe's difference in the distance traveled on their latest excursions? What if in a business session he was outvoted by a man whose taxes were a fraction of his own?

Isn't there a tinge of pride in one who has more wealth than the poor man? Most likely there is. Paul made it plain that those who are wealthy should not be "highminded."

The wealthy believer should not count too heavily on his money — "Wealth, which is so uncertain" can be lost so quickly. Even as this is written, I think of several people who were considered to be multimillionaires who now have filed for bankruptcy. Someone has put it, "Be kind to those you meet on the way up because you may meet them again on the way down."

The wealthy believer should "do good." — The implication here is that one should use that which he has to do good. There are things which the wealthy man can accomplish that could never be achieved by the poor. This, of course, is set in contrast to the one who covets wealth so he may enhance his own posture in power, honor, or still other ways. Paul requests those who have wealth not to think in terms of what they can do for themselves but rather what they can do for others. This is in perfect agreement with biblical teachings found elsewhere that the believer should always be ready to help others.

Sharing with others is a practice recommended for the rich, but it should start with those who have not yet achieved wealth, or indeed may never obtain it. It is a mentality that should characterize everyone who knows the Lord. Earlier Paul quoted Jesus' statement that it was more blessed to give than to receive (see

Acts 20:35). Happy is the person who thinks of how to give to others instead of how he may get from others.

I would strongly urge every believer to think of avenues of giving to others. He'll find an indescribable joy in such a pursuit. It may not come easy at first. There may not be that desire to give, or there may not be the evident opportunity to give. However, a commitment to give will bring the opportunity. God will provide a need if first there is that prayerful commitment to give. What better compliment could be paid a believer than that he is a "do-gooder?" God is honored by the person whose life is one series of good deeds after another. Here Paul reminds the wealthy person that he has an unmatched opportunity to do good. His wealth can provide medical aid for those who are sick, warm clothing for those who are cold, food for those who are hungry, tuition for the student, a missionary for the people waiting to hear the gospel. Paul asked Timothy to counsel the rich to be attentive to doing good for others.

Closely associated with the above are the words that *the believer should be willing to share with others, ". . . to be generous and willing to share. . ." (1 Tim. 6:18, NIV).* These words have an arresting meaning. They are translated from the word used elsewhere in the New Testament to mean "fellowship." So, it seems to speak to the rich who would seek to draw a circle around their lives and avoid contact with those who have less material possessions. The rich may be inclined to move in more tightly drawn social perimeters and allow only other wealthy people to be their companions. Paul advised Timothy to instruct those with wealth to maintain communion and fellowship with one another, never to lose sight of those in need, and always to be ready to share their resources with others.

The wealthy believer should lay up treasures in heaven, "In this way they will lay up treasure for themselves as a firm foundation for the coming age" (v. 19, NIV). — It may be that verse 19 expresses the result of verse 18, instead of a separate admonition. Either way, there is a glorious reminder for the wealthy person that his use of riches can provide wealth that will go before him into the life hereafter.

This is an overwhelming thought to me, yet one I fear few of us have considered. Oh, we have read it all right, both here and in the teachings of Jesus. But have we grasped it? Have we really understood the brevity of life here as compared to eternity? And have we realized that the medium of exchange here and the medium of exchange there are not necessarily the same? And have we realized that the transfer of funds can be made from here to there but only as we use the money here for the glory of God?

So, if this is true, I can look at my possessions, great or small, and determine whether I want them to be a temporal investment or an eternal investment. With my checkbook in hand, I can decide whether to invest in personal comforts and pleasures that will last maybe for a few years, or I can transfer it to heavenly currency and send it on to glory by giving here and now to Him.

And the rich person is so fortunate that he has such a golden opportunity with his great wealth to invest abundantly in the life hereafter.

The wealthy believer should remember that wealth has been given by God for man's enjoyment, "God, who giveth us richly all things to enjoy" (v. 17, KJV). —This is not a conflict with earlier statements about wealth; neither does it say that either much or little is better or more spiritual. Spirituality is not to be equated with either, but I do think that many often have the mistaken idea that God is a hardened tyrant who is looking for ways to hurt His children and to keep them from being happy. No! Indeed not! God is not looking for ways to hurt us — He is looking for ways to help us. Of course, in our lack of maturity, even as it is with a small child, we are not ready to receive His gifts, but surely God loves His children more than any earthly father could love his. Any earthly father who loves his children is not looking for ways to hurt or deprive his children. Because he loves them, he is looking for ways to help them.

Likewise, God loves His children and wants to provide for their happiness, and if God chooses to bless with wealth, it should not be scorned and looked upon as evil. It should be received with thanksgiving and with the determination that it will be used for His glory. After all, it is not the possession of wealth that is evil; it is what one does with wealth that makes it right or wrong.

−6−

Dreaming of Paradise
The Goal of the Steward

I confess that I approach this section with some difficulty. Where is the goal of the steward clearly defined or described? If we casually disregard the teachings of Paul we would possibly answer the question by affirming that the goal of the steward is to ascertain the will and wishes of his Master and to execute faithfully every wish with joy and effectiveness, and who is to claim that is not true?

But what does Paul really indicate to be the goal of the believer? Where does he spell out such a goal? Some would say that Paul expresses it in Philippians 3:14 where it is called, "the prize of the high calling of God in Christ Jesus" (KJV), and who is to argue it is not? Others may feel it is expressed in Philippians 1:21, "For to me to live is Christ, and to die is gain" (KJV), and I would certainly be slow to counter that.

It seems to me that these can be ruled out on the basis of a fine-line distinction in which both of these speak of an ultimate achievement and not an ongoing stewardship experience. Granted, Philippians 1:21 also could be that ongoing experience,

85

but it seems to be a holy commitment as distinguished from a battle-by-battle, day-by-day, acceptable relationship of the steward with his master. So, I want to suggest that the stewardship goal for which every believer should strive, whether young or old, rich or poor, male or female, regardless of race is "contentment."

Paul used the word "contentment" only three times. In Philippians 4:11, it is translated "content," in 1 Tim. 6:6, "contentment," and in 2 Corinthians 9:8, "all sufficiency."

So, in this concluding part, I want to enlarge upon "contentment, the goal of the steward," and discuss it under four headings:

(1) The meaning of contentment;

(2) The example of contentment;

(3) The achievement of contentment; and

(4) The fruits of contentment.

The Meaning of Contentment.

The Greek word translated in each of the Scripture references is one used to describe a condition in life that is perfect and where one has no need for support or assistance in any way.

This is why I have chosen to call it the *goal* of the steward. The steward is perfectly satisfied with his calling, pleased with his wages. He has no apprehension about what he will live on tomorrow. He has absolute trust in the sufficiency and provision of God. He responds to invest or to give exactly what the Master asks of him. He is able to put first things first and last things last. He accepts a morsel of bread with gratitude. He accepts the bounty of affluence with commitment. That man has achieved faithful stewardship, and he is a contented man.

In Paul's day the Stoics believed that one would be able to achieve contentment only as he reduced his desires. Remove the desires and the level of satisfaction would be obtainable, but man's reducing his desires to achieve contentment should be distinguished from the contentment of which Paul speaks, a serenity wherein God gives peace and contentment without fear and apprehension or covetousness and greed.

If the steward sizes up his lot in life as his own personal achievement, then he may well be frustrated and confused, and that frustration will come when he does or does not reach his goals, because they are *his* goals. If he fails to reach them, he blames himself, and in his strength tries harder. If he reaches his goals, he discovers only that his greed has increased. Soon, he has fallen into the snare of foolish and hurtful lusts and so-called "contentment" is only a pathetic wish of a frustrated life.

But contentment can come only to the believer who is committed to the control of God over his life. In such a commitment, he has the assurance that he is doing what God wants done, where He wants it done, and is receiving the wages which are right for his doing it.

From this, one should never conclude that I am contending for a passive existence for the believer. No! I do not believe that God sets one down in the world like a spring-driven toy that has wound down. But I insist that after one has intently pursued the goals God has led him to set for his life, he should be perfectly at peace and without fear and frustration. In fact, in Paul's usage of the word in this letter to the Corinthians, he speaks of contentment as the prelude to one's effective service. "And God is able to make all grace abound toward you; that ye, always having all sufficiency [contentment] in all things, may abound to every good work" (2 Cor. 9:8, KJV, author's brackets). Contentment is the preface to one's abounding in every good work.

The Example of Contentment

Paul was grateful for all he had received.

> But I have all, and abound: I am full, having received of Epaphroditus the things which were sent from you, an odor of a sweet smell, a sacrifice

acceptable, well pleasing unto God (Phil. 4:18, KJV).

The NIV translates the earlier part of this verse, "I have received full payment and even more," which lends some credence to the interpretation that the Philippians were paying a debt to Paul. However, I do not believe that was his point at all. His bookkeeping terminology did not mean that the Philippians had paid their statement in full and thereby were relieved of any further accountability. Instead, Paul was expressing his personal and deep gratitude for every abundance God had given.

How easy it would have been for Paul to have complained and lamented the unfortunate circumstances of his condition. He was incarcerated in a Roman prison cell, even though there was no felony charge against him. He was limited to prison rations, even though he had brought offense to no one. He could have asked why it was that he, a scholar, an apostle, a missionary, a beloved preacher, a pioneer of the Christian faith, who should have enjoyed the honor, devotion, and support of his friends, was found instead to be jailed as a common prisoner.

There was no such complaint from Paul. He had assurance he was doing God's will, so he had no lamentation for any suffering that might come his way. His words to the Philippians were not intended to imply that they had paid their debt in full but that his needs were met in full. In him there was no greed or covetousness for more and more of the things of this world. Instead, there was contentment (Phil. 4:11) because he had come to accept with complete satisfaction and gratitude, that which had come to him in response to his being in the center of God's will. It was this kind of contentment that could enable Paul to testify of himself in such moving language, "as having nothing, and yet possessing all things" (2 Cor. 6:10, KJV).

He had reached contentment by growth. — "For I have learned, in whatsoever state I am, therewith to be content" (Phil. 4:11, KJV). For one brief moment Paul digs out of his past to share an incomplete testimony about himself. Yet, despite the brevity of that testimony, it ignites explosions of conjecture. What did Paul mean, "I have learned"? What experiences out of the past had mellowed his aspirations, rectified his ambitions, and cradled his satisfaction? If the truth were known, I believe that Paul thought back over many years to recurring and alternating experiences of hurt, praise, joy, disappointment, success, and failure – and therein found the gradual molding of a life that found contentment. It had not developed in an instant; he had learned it. It was not a gift from above; he had learned it. It was not a story he read of another; he had learned it. It was step by step, whereby he grew into the wonderful likeness of Jesus (see 2 Cor. 3:18).

The Achievement of Contentment.

In the following outline I admit there are suggestions which are purely personal. I will not necessarily cite chapter and verse from Paul's writings to confirm them. However, I do feel that they are drawn from the body of Pauline material and are appropriate instructions for the believer who would seek to find the illusive gem of contentment. Much of the material has been discussed to some degree in earlier portions of this writing, so I will endeavor to avoid unnecessary and repetitive remarks.

One should know that his life is in the will and purpose of God. – Until He returns, there can be little contentment if there is the constant fear that one should be in another place and doing something different.

One should reflect a grateful heart. – Instead of the ceaseless greed which asks, "Why don't I have more?" contentment is nourished in the spirit of "I am grateful and blessed to have what I have."

One should walk by faith. – Knowing that God owns it all, and that what we have is from Him keeps us from wondering why there is not more. No doubt the greatest body of material ever to be written on this is found in Paul's second letter to the Corinthians. Who of us has not read and heard quoted, "For we walk by faith, not by sight"? (2 Cor. 5:7, KJV). But verse 7 cannot be appreciated without reading a portion of the Letter prior to that verse. Beginning with 4:8 in the same translation, Paul gives a long list of bad things that come to the believer but he follows each with a contrasting good thing that follows each bad. He first says. . .

> We are troubled on every side, yet not distressed (v. 8); We are perplexed, but not in despair (v. 8); Persecuted, but not forsaken (v. 9); Cast down, but not destroyed (v. 9); . . .we. . .are always delivered unto death. . . knowing that he which raised up the Lord Jesus shall raise up us also. . .(vv. 11,14); . . . though our outward man perish, yet the inward man is renewed (v. 16); . . .if our earthly house. . . were dissolved, we have a building of God . . .eternal in the heavens (5:1).

And then Paul expresses his hope and expectations in the Lord. "Our affliction is light and is but for a moment" (4:17). "We look beyond the temporal things to the eternal" (4:18).

Having read these lofty statements of courage and hope, one wants to inquire, "How, Paul? How can you express such confidence, such hope, such acceptance, and such expectancy?" Paul answers in verse 7, "For we walk by faith, not by sight." Here the word "For" carries the meaning in this structure of "because." It is as if a boy is asking his confident friend, "Why did you do that?" to which the boy simply answers, "Cause."

We read Paul's statement of confidence and hope and respond with loud and plaintive concern, "How, Paul," to which Paul simply responds, "Because we walk by faith, not by sight" (5:7).

One should not let greed acquire what would create a disturbing indebtedness. — This statement may appear to be very casual, but remember we are talking about the secret to contentment.

Earlier we discussed the impropriety of greed for the Christian steward. It nurtures ingratitude, ruthlessness, and a selfishness which boasts that one deserves what he has and more. Observe also that greed often is the reason for one's buying more and more and more until there is no capacity to pay for it, or it is paid for at the neglect of other essentials. Then comes the unhappiness with one's companion, unhappiness with one's job, unhappiness with the Lord, and unhappiness with oneself, and the subsequent neglect of all of the above. Thus, contentment has died on that burning desert of greed.

One should avoid an envy that would cause strife. – This, too, has been discussed earlier as an evil of unfaithful stewardship. One who gives to God sparingly, grudgingly, and of compulsion (2 Cor. 9:6) is that person who selfishly retains for himself that he may gain security, independence, and power, which, of course, often sets up a collision course with friends, or relatives, or neighbors. Instead of gratitude for the blessings of God, one envies another who seems to have what he has been unable in his own power to attain.

One should give faithfully to maintain a heart of unselfishness. – Without this, one is doomed to discontentment. I repeat: Jesus declared that it is more blessed to give than to receive. Happier is the person and more contented is the person who looks for ways to give, rather than looking for ways to receive.

The person who, through selfishness, keeps what he has is always looking for how to acquire more and is never content or happy with what he has. By giving one learns the joy of giving, and he continues to give, knowing well the source of his blessings. Knowing the source of his blessings, he is content with whatever God places into his hand.

The selfish heart is never satisfied, never content. The unselfish heart is grateful for its own blessings and content with whatever comes its way. Surely none had given more than Paul, and it was he who confessed, "I am amply supplied" (Phil. 4:18, NIV).

One should learn to forget. – In Philippians 3:13, Paul begins to name what he would do until the coming of the Lord in order to "apprehend" that for which he was "apprehended," and he starts with the fact that he would forget those things which were behind. Good advice!

Maybe one would reply that you can't merely wipe something out of your mind, to which I would readily agree. One might also be advised that he should not keep calling back the past and mentally rehashing it again and again. To recall it, retain it, and worry about it will keep it as a mental roadblock to stand in the path of better and more delightful blessings.

To forget the past one can do at least three things. One, mentally dismiss the matter and simply refuse to think further about it. Second, replace it with something good. If it was an unpleasant event, substitute it with a pleasant one. If there was a demoralizing failure, forget it and think about the victories. If there is an unsavory person who plagues your thinking, substitute the worry with an act of kindness. Three, remind yourself that this will be so inconsequential as time removes you further away from it. So, until then, don't let worry destroy you. That is a victory Satan does not deserve.

Don't pursue vengeance to settle the score. —There can be no contentment while you scheme to settle the score with another. "But I was wronged," you might argue. Maybe you were; maybe you were not. Information is not always accurate.

Even if you were wronged, that does not give you the right to hurt someone in return. If you have been wronged, God will take care of it. Paul makes that plain in Romans 12:19, "Dearly beloved, avenge not yourselves, but rather give place unto wrath: for it is written, vengeance is mine; I will repay saith the Lord." Simply put, God charges us, "You leave this alone; if you have been wronged, back off and let Me take care of it." And He will. When Haman prepared a gallows on which to hang innocent Mordecai, God reversed the plan, and Haman was hanged on his own gallows.

When his critics finally did Daniel wrong and had him thrown to the lions, God seized control and reversed the plan. Daniel was not hurt, but his accusers were thrown to the lions where they and their families were immediately destroyed.

Judas sold Jesus for thirty pieces of silver, God raised Jesus from the dead, and Judas was buried on the property bought with the money he received from selling Jesus.

When one has been wronged, there is often a passion to "get even." Yet the greatest evidence of strength is in the quiet contentment to believe, "God will take care of it."

One should determine to help others (see Phil. 2:4 and James 2:15-17). — It was pointed out earlier that greed is the enemy of contentment. To hoard for oneself is to intensify restlessness and discontent. The prevailing cry of "more, more" will rob any heart of peace and never allow the warm waters of contentment to bathe and caress the tense muscles of one's soul. Whereas a morsel of bread for the hungry, a blanket for one that is cold, or a ticket home for the stranded will go far to erase an uptight spirit and settle the anxious heart into an attitude of tranquillity and contentment.

Even though there is an effort to stay with the epistles of Paul, the next two will be taken from the Gospel of Matthew. From Matthew 6:25-34, one learns the importance of accepting the provision of God. — Once and again (verses 25 and 31) Jesus counsels His hearers that they take no thought (do not worry) about the basics of food and clothing. He reminds them of His care for the frail birds, so surely He can care for them. He reminds them that they can't extend their lives, so why worry about life? He further reminds them that he adorns flowers with beauty that eludes the riches of man, so why do they worry about their bodies? Jesus desires so intensely that His disciples live in the joy of contentment and escape the debilitating pains of anxiety.

The other from Jesus is that we simply *accept His love.* — Read again Matthew 7:7-11. Jesus promised to hear us as we pray, and that promise should stand from God unaided, but Jesus doesn't leave it there. He chided His disciples by reminding them that as earthly parents they love their children enough that they would not give to them a stone if they asked for bread, they would not give them a serpent if they asked for a fish. As parents, hopefully they would not do anything but good for their children. So do you think for a moment, he asked, that the Heavenly Father would do less for His children?

So, why the anxiety? Why the care? Why the fear? Why the tension? Why sell your soul short of its promised peace? Why shred your nocturnal retreat with spasms of worry? God desires for you to have contentment. God consoles you, "Why worry about it? I love you!"

The Fruits of Contentment.

What are the blessings which contentment brings? Once again, I want to share some personal observations which are, at least indirectly, supported in the teachings of Paul.

Contentment allows restful nerves since one will not be greedily trying to be like others. —How sad it is to see someone who constantly must be trying to match or excel someone else. They cannot look at another's new home without returning home in frustration to conjure up some way to make theirs the same. They cannot enjoy another's new clothes, car, or even his child's education without frustration over their own failure to be able to match them. A common example of this is one who pretends not to want a specific item at all, when the truth is he is extremely frustrated over being unable to match or exceed it. Contentment avoids that kind of frustration.

Contentment allows more thought for worthy pursuits. —This is an immediate successor to the one preceding. If one is content, with no frustrated thoughts about how he can match or exceed his friend or neighbor, then he can concentrate on more worthy pursuits. And I am not merely suggesting that if five minutes are not spent on keeping up with the Joneses, then there are a surplus five minutes to think worthy thoughts. In simple subtraction that may be true, but psychologically it is much more than that. Thought that is spent on the frustration of being unable to match the Joneses is not just measured in minutes, it is measured in lives — lives that are happy, peaceful, and that are loved, as over against lives that are cynical, sad, bitter, and shunned by others.

A life that is spent being measured by someone else will ultimately show the awful price that has been paid. It will not only shape an attitude and disposition, it will also mold one's life and one's countenance.

In my study, I have a sculpture, made in an art class, of an Indian head that was given to me by my daughter, Jan. I treasure it because of how I got it but also because of what seems to my untrained eye to be a rather accurate reproduction. Each time I look at that old Indian, I wonder what were the worries he must have borne and which have molded his countenance.

So contentment allows one to think more creatively and responsibly about intellectual pursuits, social interests, spiritual needs, or even pleasure.

Contentment issues in more thanksgiving than would be found with those in more selfish pursuits. — It seems reasonable to assume that if one is not content, then he will not give gratitude to God who gave him that which has caused discontent. Human nature is such that we express thanksgiving for whatever pleases us, and if one is not content or pleased with what he has, he is not likely to joyfully express thanksgiving for it.

So, contentment gives rise to that noble gesture of thanksgiving that Paul considered pivotal for the believer. In his instructions to the Philippians he counseled, "Do not be anxious about anything, but in everything, by prayer and petition, with thanksgiving, present your request to God" (Phil. 4:6, NIV). And to the Colossians he wrote,

> So then, just as you receive Christ Jesus as Lord,
> continue to live in him, rooted and built up in him,
> strengthened in the faith as you were taught, and
> overflowing with thankfulness (Col. 2:6-7, NIV).

So, a good practice for the believer is to delay the asking part of his prayer time until he has first engaged in the thanksgiving period. God surely must be pleased that, after we have asked Him for specific things and they are given to us, we care enough to tell Him of our gratitude. But, conversely, there is very little gratitude from a heart filled with discontentment.

Contentment contributes to integrity in relationships. — Without the greed of discontent, one does not need to overprice or underweigh or to mistreat other workers. Only a few months ago a leading national magazine featured a number of well-known and highly respected individuals who had been indicted in crimes against their fellowman, most of which were directly or indirectly related to greed.

Where are we going? Is the American dream now only obtainable through a disregard for one's fellowman? Do men peddle drugs that wreck the lives of good people just to satisfy their material discontent? Do legislators vote without regard for integrity because they want the flow of financial support not to dry up? Do companies say whatever is necessary in their ads to dupe another customer to buy their product and thereby enrich their coffers? Have we even in churches resorted to methods alone to achieve power in numbers and financial support because of an insatiable hunger and ungodly discontent? It seems that all of these and so many more are sadly true because man has not found contentment in God.

This part may appropriately be summed up in a verse from Hebrews which may or may not be the work of Paul. "Let your conversation be without covetousness; and be content with such things as you have: for he hath said, I will never leave thee, nor forsake thee" (Heb. 13:5).

It is so clearly evident that there are two basic essentials for contentment, namely, one should have faith in God who said "I will never leave thee nor forsake thee." One does not seek contentment. One follows after those factors which make for contentment, and thereafter finds the luscious fruit which grew from the seeds of his commitment.

Shakespeare expressed it so well in *King Henry VI*:

> My Crown is in my heart, not on my head;
> Not deck'd with diamonds and Indian Stones;
> Nor to be seen: My Crown is called Content;
> A Crown it is that seldom kings enjoy.
> (Part III, Act III, Scene 1)

Conclusion

There is no desire, intent, or effort to draw up a long list of summary conclusions about Paul's teaching on stewardship, but there are a couple of matters I must mention. First, Paul never refers directly to the tithe. The reasons for this may be more obvious to some and less obvious to others. Regardless of the reasons, his failure to mention it does not mean he did not believe or practice it. Surely his training had brought him to accept such a practice and had he rejected it as a Christian and believed it was wrong, it is reasonable to assume he would have denounced it, even as he did other forms of legalism, in his Letter to the Galatians. Paul certainly was not averse to expressing his opposition to what he did not believe.

Even though Paul does not directly refer to the tithe, it should be observed that he did refer to percentage giving, at least indirectly. In his instructions to the Corinthians, he did prescribe, "Upon the first day of the week let every one of you lay by him in store, as God hath prospered him, that there be no gatherings when I come" (1 Cor. 16:2, KJV).

It has been argued that Paul does not emphasize regular church support in this passage because the chapter begins by referring to the benevolence offering for the poor believers. It is true that such a reference is made. Regardless of that, the offering was to be a weekly offering, and it was to be according to one's prosperity.

One's giving according to prosperity can only be interpreted as percentage giving if taken very literally. And if this is to be taken in such a literal manner, then Paul does make reference to percentage giving and perhaps to the tithe.

Second, Paul speaks of a higher relationship. I think that Paul wrote of a higher relationship that causes one to give from a regenerated heart, not less but perhaps more. This he expressed in Ephesians 2:8-10, where he declared we were saved by grace and created unto good works in which God had ordained that we walk. Or as he wrote to the Philippians, "my earnest expectation . . . that . . . Christ shall be magnified in my body" (Phil. 1:20, KJV). And it is expressed in that familiar passage in 2 Corinthians, "Every man according as he purposeth in his heart, so let him give" (2 Cor. 9:7, KJV).

Paul's mind probably thought of the days of his fathers in Egypt when they gave service in the brick kilns of the Egyptian lords, but not from a willing heart. It was not from a heart of love and gratitude, but it was service and labor at the end of a whip. Now Paul saw a relationship in giving that grew out of redemption by Him who, though He was rich, yet for our sakes He became poor, that we through His poverty might be rich (2 Cor. 8:9). With Paul it would be a new dimension of giving, emanating from a new relationship with God.

I think it would be appropriate to conclude a work on Paul's view of stewardship by taking an incisive look at Paul himself. And after one has done this, I think all that Paul has written about stewardship will come more clearly into focus. For this picture of Paul, I should like to forego what others have said about him and go directly to what Paul said about himself.

I am not only interested in his comments concerning his personal qualities. That would be too subjective. Rather, how did Paul label himself and what did Paul think of other people? Thereby we might formulate a rather accurate and objective picture of what he himself was. And, interestingly enough, it is all found in one chapter of his writings. It is in Romans 1, and I shall limit myself to an outline and will suggest that the reader "flesh out" the bones.

I. Paul's View of Himself (1:1)

A. He was a servant (1:1).

B. He was an apostle (1:1).

C. He was anointed (1:1).

II. Paul's View of Jesus (1:3-5)

A. He is man — "seed of David according to the flesh" (1:3).

B. He is God — "Son of God...according to the Spirit"(1:4).

C. He is mediator — "By whom we have received..." (1:5).

III. Paul's View of Fellow Believers — "beloved of God" (1:7).

A. He was thankful for them (1:8).

B. He prayed for them (1:9).

C. He was concerned about their growth (1:11).

D. He desired mutual benefit from them (1:12).

IV. Paul's View of the Lost (1:14-15).

A. He was debtor to them (1:14).

B. He was ready to go to them (1:15).

A man's view of himself and what he thinks of others will give a fairly accurate picture about the quality of a person and the life he lives. So it is with the above, and I shall let it stand at that.

Perhaps it would be impossible to read of the exhortations and noble examples given by Paul on stewardship without feeling that proper stewardship is a goal too high and too holy to claim. It is so far to go from point A to point B. But I must come to state in these concluding remarks that it is not accomplished in one giant leap. Instead, it is reached little bit by little bit as we grow more and more into the likeness of Jesus.

To illustrate this, I will tell of an experience in closing this study.

Several years ago the condition of my Dad's health required rather serious surgery for which he was transferred to the old Baptist Hospital in Jackson, Mississippi. Several of us children joined our mother at the hospital on the morning of the surgery and stayed there until Dad was back in his room. At that time I suggested that the others return to their homes for a brief rest, and I would sit with Dad because on the next day I would have to return to my home, leaving his care in the hands of those who lived nearby.

I had brought along a book from my library and was enjoying a quiet reading time when I was impressed by the translation of a verse of Scripture given by the author. I reread it a few times and then went on to his subsequent material.

After a while I decided to leave Dad asleep and walk down the hall for a bit of relaxation. I walked to the hospital lobby and turned to go back to Dad's room when I was stricken by the portraits hanging on the wall. I assumed that they were benefactors of the hospital and were surely husband and wife. But I was somewhat startled to see that they resembled each other. Then after a moment of staring at this elderly couple who "favored" each other, I rushed back down the hall to read again the verse I had paused to observe a bit earlier. And there it was, "And we all, with unveiled face, beholding the glory of the Lord, are being changed into his likeness from one degree of glory to another" (2 Cor. 3:18, RSV).

I did not at the time know what translation the author had used, but I later discovered that it was the *Revised Standard Version*. As I read that, and as I remembered the portraits down the hall, I recalled something I had heard many times — that two people can live together long enough until they begin to resemble each other. That was the situation with the couple in the portraits, and it was what Paul was saying about our relationship with Jesus. The maturing or "likeness" process is not instantaneous; it is gradual. But if we keep our eyes on Him, it will happen.

In this verse (2 Cor. 3:18), Paul first had acknowledged our saving relationship with Jesus in the words "with unveiled face" (review the previous verses of the chapter). Then he spoke of "beholding" or "fastening one's eyes" upon Jesus. Following this he said that we "are being changed," which is a gradual and continuous process, "from one degree of glory to another." There it was in the inspired writings of Paul . . . if I have been saved and if I will fasten my heart and eyes upon Jesus, then I shall be changed into His likeness one degree at a time, not suddenly, but one degree at a time.

As I sat there, I recalled the classic novel written by Hawthorne, *The Great Stone Face*. The setting, as I recalled it, was a small New England farming village nestled in a valley between the mountains. Generations remained to farm the valley, and all heard repeated the legend of the "great stone face."

All the people knew and had seen on one of the mountains a face that looked remarkably like that of a man, and a legend had been told that one day one of the young men would be the great stone face.

Again and again the young men left the valley to make their fortunes in the world and in the course of time would return to visit the place of their birth. Upon such visits, the villagers would always compare them with the great stone face, only to express the same repeated disappointment.

There also was born in the valley a little boy named Ernest, and he, too, as a young lad, had heard the legend of the great stone face. While working in his father's field he would often pause to look at the mountain and think, *One day, someone will look like the great stone face.*

When Ernest reached maturity, he married and settled in the valley where he cultivated his own field as a young adult, a middleaged father, and as an aging grandfather. All through those years, Ernest would pause, gaze upon the stone face, and remember the legend. This continued until he was an old man, and then one day the people looked at him and exclaimed, "Ernest is the great stone face!" He had gazed upon it until he had become like it.

So Hawthorne, Paul, the portraits in Baptist Hospital, and the stories I had heard all taught the same truth—if you gaze upon the one you love, you will, degree by degree, grow to be like the object of your love. It is not an instant maturity—it is a gradual process.

One day I was in the Dallas-Fort Worth International Airport waiting for my flight departure, and I went to use the telephone located on the wall of a busy concourse of the airport. As I used the phone I was able to casually watch the busy flow of people who passed nearby. All was rather routine until I observed coming my way a couple who surely must have been husband and wife. They were getting on in years, and I was stricken by the fact that they resembled each other. Are you surprised that when I lowered my eyes I saw, and not really to my surprise—they were holding hands!

Other Books by Douglas L. Laird

Why Worry? Wit & Wisdom From Proverbs
Do you want insight into the world's problems? Understanding of the human condition? Answers to personal, family, economic, political, and societal issues? And would you like to have those at your fingertips even before the media jump on them? Then there is a Book, written centuries ago, that is more up-to-date than tomorrow's morning newspaper — the Book of Proverbs in the Bible! Laird has combed that ancient, yet remarkably contemporary book and drawn together vignettes of amazing wisdom.

Don't Talk to Me About Giving
In this book, the author does exactly opposite of what the title states. He does talk about giving and lists ten common excuses expressed by those who give little or nothing. After grappling with these excuses, his final conclusions are that giving is a blessing, not a curse. This small book is an excellent resource for distribution among church members during the annual stewardship emphasis.

Stewardship Sermon Outlines, Volumes I, II, III
Outstanding, practical, workable, usable sermon outlines for the busy pastor as he plans his pulpit ministry.

Order from

Christian Stewardship Ministries
4406 N. Perryville Road
Litchfield Park, AZ 85340
1-800-926-4891